WRITING ESSENTIALS

(ACADEMIC AND GENERAL – STRATEGIES, SKILLS & ESSENTIALS)

Jyoti Malhotra
(B.A Hons. M.A., NET-1, E-Commerce)

Published by:

F-2/16, Ansari road, Daryaganj, New Delhi-110002
☎ 23240026, 23240027 • *Fax:* 011-23240028
Email: info@vspublishers.com • *Website:* www.vspublishers.com
Online Brandstore: *amazon.in/vspublishers*

Regional Office : Hyderabad
5-1-707/1, Brij Bhawan (Beside Central Bank of India Lane)
Bank Street, Koti, Hyderabad - 500 095
☎ 040-24737290
E-mail: vspublishershyd@gmail.com

Follow us on:   

BUY OUR BOOKS FROM: AMAZON FLIPKART

ISBN 978-93-505712-6-2
New Edition

Printed at : Param Offsetters, Okhla, New Delhi–110020

Dedication

I, with due respect and profound privilege, serene dignity and folded hands dedicate my small piece of research program to my devoted and dedicated parents, Mrs. Kiran Malhotra and Mr. Pradeep Malhotra for their wholesome support and their dignified ambience which they offered me to sail the boat of my life on the path of hardwork and determination. I am really very thankful to both of them for blooming my life with their humble ambience.

Acknowledgement

There is a big vote bank of thanks in my whole projection of this project to my worthy parents, Mrs. & Mr. Deep Birla, My Guide, Mr. Parminder Singh Bhogal, Caring Brothers & Sisters - Mrs. & Mr. Rohit Gandhi, Mrs. & Mr. Aman Malhotra and Mrs. & Mr. Sandeep Malhotra.

My heartiest thanks to my life partner, Mr. Deepak Malhotra (husband) and the little steps of my Angel, Ditya Malhotra (daughter).

I am really grateful to be a part of the V & S Publishers who support my research analysis with their expert team of publishing. I am really very thankful to Mr. Sahil Gupta (Director) and Mr. Binay Srivastava for their wholesome cooperation to convert my research program to a complete masterpiece.

Regards

Jyoti Malhotra

Publisher's Note

V&S Publishers has recently ventured into the field of *Academic Books* with the launch of the *Gen X Series*. 'Gen X' stands for 'Excellence in Generation 'X'. The series comprises books for aspirants of various competitive examinations. Hence, following the success of our previous books in this series, we decided to launch a **series of IELTS or the International English Language Testing System books** under this series. The subject has been divided into five main parts which has been grouped into five books by the author, such as: ***IELTS Tech-Academic Module***, ***IELTS Tech-Writing Essentials***, ***IELTS Tech-Vocal Cosmetics***, ***IELTS Tech- General Module*** and ***IELTS Tech- Speaking Essentials*** for the students, who aspire to study, work or settle abroad.

The books in this exclusive Series are written especially for the Indian students who wish to appear in the IELTS exams. Most of the foreign books available in the market on this subject have been written keeping in view the foreign readers and at times, may appear *Greek* to the students from India, primarily because of issues related to accent, grammatical aspects, spellings, etc. Therefore, the need for these books was felt by V&S Publishers and the author's extensive research on this subject was carefully moulded to present it in the form of five perfect books on IELTS, specifically for Indian students.

Each book contains **Skills, Strategies and Guidelines** written in a simple manner along with Youtube video (Dropbox link given below) that accompanies the book which is also one of the unique features of this Series. The **Youtube viedo is interactive and illustrative** and presented in a manner that even an average student can grasp the contents and master the language easily and quickly. So, V&S Publishers hopes that through these books, we can offer the IELTS aspirants--**A Smarter Way to Learn Technical English nationwide.**

Access Conent Online on Dropbox: https://www.dropbox.com/sh/ojfu6ppzu9ki37l/AADOzihXybFClIIm09TTo_rpa?dl=0

Contents

Preface

IELTS- TECH - A complete Toolkit for learning, practising and knowing about IELTS. As the world is growing smarter, the ways of its learning and getting education also gets smarter day by day. IELTS-TECH (A TECHNICAL TOOLKIT OF LEARNING INTERNATIONAL LANGUAGE TESTING SYSTEM) is also acting as a smarter way to learn IELTS via Presentations on its strategies. This toolkit completely clarifies four sections.

Reading:

This refers to the IELTS aspirants' development in reading, understanding and responding to a wide range of spoken, written and visual English texts. It involves learners' developing understandings of how texts are organised and how language varies according to the situation, social and cultural contexts, purpose and audience.

Writing:

It refers to the IELTS aspirants' development in writing a range of texts for interpersonal, informational and aesthetic purposes. It involves developing writing skills including task response, Coherence, Lexical Resource and Grammar skills

Speaking:

This refers the IELTS aspirants' development in using spoken Standard English for communication for social and school-based learning. It involves developing learners' control over Standard English phonology, word and sentence stress, rhythm and intonation and the information conveyed by these systems.

Listening:

It refers to the IELTS aspirants' development in understanding spoken Standard English. It focusses on the ability to actively listen for a

purpose and involves learners being able to select and apply strategies to make meaning in a wide range of contexts.

IELTS TECH SERVES THE YOUNG ASPIRANTS WITH ITS TOOLKIT OF FIVE BOOKS

BOOK 1 : IELTS -Tech : It includes Reading, Writing, Speaking, and Listening along with its strategies to crack with the practice sessions.

BOOK 2 : WRITING ESSENTIALS : It will serve the Academic and General candidates with writing topics. This book covers the wide range of Graphical Representation, General letters and few Academic and General topics of writing.

BOOK 3 : VOCAL COSMETICS AND SPEECH THERAPY FOR IELTS: This book will enhance the speaking skills of the candidate. Students will come to know the technical aspect in IELTS related to speaking techniques like Word Stress, Intonation, Rhythm, Coherence, Lexical Resource, Fluency, etc.

BOOK 4 : GENERAL MODULE FOR IELTS This book will help the general candidate who are appearing for IELTS. It covers Reading, Writing, Speaking and Listening skills with strategies and practice sessions.

BOOK 5 : SPEAKING ESSENTIALS : This will serve both the Academic and General candidates regarding interview sessions between interviewer and interviewee. It covers PART-1 Personal Interaction, PART-2 Cue -Cards, PART-3 Follow up Session.

SPECIAL ATTRACTION IN IELTS – TECH

AWARENESS SESSIONS : These powerpoint smart sessions will help the students to build their ideology towards simple topics like Education, Media, Music, Technology, Tourism, Culture, Science, Computers, Health, etc. These awareness sessions is an endeavour to raise the standards of vocabulary and terminology of the aspirants. This will enhance the lexical resource for Writing and Speaking skills. These awareness sessions not only serves Vocabulary Usage but also provides Traditional and Contemporary Outlook, Quotations and Proverbial Matter, Author Sayings, Volley of Idioms and Phrases related to it… etc. This Youtube video will be provided with the Writing Essentials and Speaking Essentials.

SMART CD OF POWERPOINT PRESENTATION : IELTS- TECH is a smart tech product which help the aspirants to understand the technicalities of the IELTS exams with visual aids. This product is the package of strategies to crack the four modules of IELTS, i.e., Reading, Writing, Speaking and Listening with its Do's and Don'ts.

COMPACT DISK OF LISTENING SESSIONS : For enhancing the listening part of the candidate, listening activities are provided in the Youtube video for their practice.

About Writing Essentials

IELTS – TECH WRITING ESSENTIALS is an answer to the writing skills for an IELTS exam. This book comprises of three sections – (i) *Graphical Representations, (ii) Letter Writing, (iii)Essays* for the IELTS Exams. Not only this, the book provides one Youtube video to make the students aware of the vocabulary of common topics, its importance in the present and the future, language usage, etc. Many practice sessions are also available for improving the writing capacity of the student.

ABSTRACT

Writing Essentials chapter one guides the students how to crack task 1 (Graphic Representation) & Task 2 (Essay writing topics) with its strategies & techniques. It clarifies strategies related to Graphs i.e. how to introduce the graph, how to comment on increasing & decreasing trends, concluding aspect of the graph along with word power i.e. vocabulary usage or lexical for writing graph. similarly this chapter also clarifies the strategies for essay writing topics with An Art of Rhetorical Devices & 'W' Family. In this way this chapter will act as a guide & first approach to deal with writing task for IELTS. Certain examples & tips are provided for the thorough understanding of the concept.

WRITING TASK – 1
GRAPHIC REPRESENTATION

It is an information transfer task related to the factual content of the input texts, graphs, tables or diagrams. Sometimes, you will have to describe a process shown in the diagram.

Strategy No. 1 : How To Introduce The Graph

- ★ Do mention in the beginning that which TYPE of graph it is. i.e., whether the graph is BAR, LINE, PIE, TABLE.
- ★ Do write the TITLE of the graph, i.e., what type of information the graph is conveying.
- ★ Do mention the DATE, MONTH & YEAR of the graph.
- ★ It is necessary to describe the SCALE of the graph, i.e., whether the graph is marked in hundreds, thousands, millions, pounds, dollars, kilograms, tons, meters, kilometers, percentage and so on…..

Strategy No. 2 : How To Describe The Graph

1. NO DETAILED DISCUSSION

No need to write the whole data, for example: there is no need to give reasons for why figures are moving low or high. No specialized knowledge or individual opinions are required.

2. DESCRIBE THE TRENDS

A trend needs to describe, i.e., how values change generally over time and it is important to describe the changes along with some sort of numerical values.

3. INCLUDE ALL THE DETAILS FOR SMALL GRAPHS

If there is only one graph and it does not have much numerical data in it, then it will be expected to include all or nearly all of the numerical details.

4. GROUPING OF GRAPHS

If there is an option with two graphs, then it is not necessary to describe every small or big detail of the numerical data as IELTS bounds the candidate with 150 words to perform the task 1. So just include the significant details which are worth mentioning and make it more reliable and stable to understand.

<u>EXAMPLES</u>

Here we are providing the examples of different types of graphs which maybe asked in the IELTS exam. With the help of the tips given along with the, graph candidates will be able to solve the problems more accurately, easily and speedily.

Example (Tips) : Line Graph

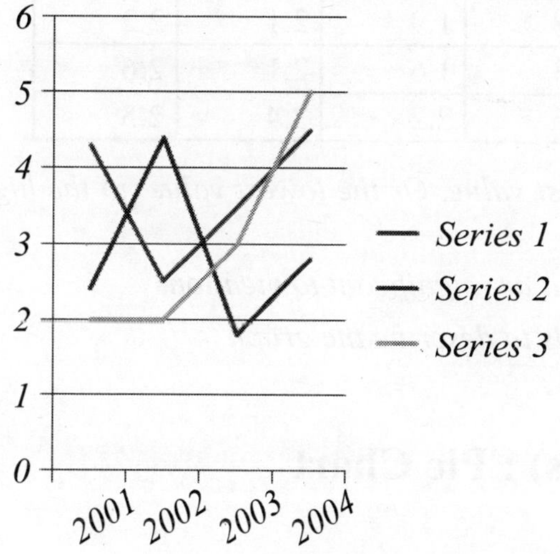

- ✯ *Describe the trend pictorically.*
- ✯ *Describe the movement of the lines of the graph giving numerical detail at the important points of the line.*
- ✯ *Use appropriate vocabulary of graphic words.*

Example (Tips) : Bar Graph

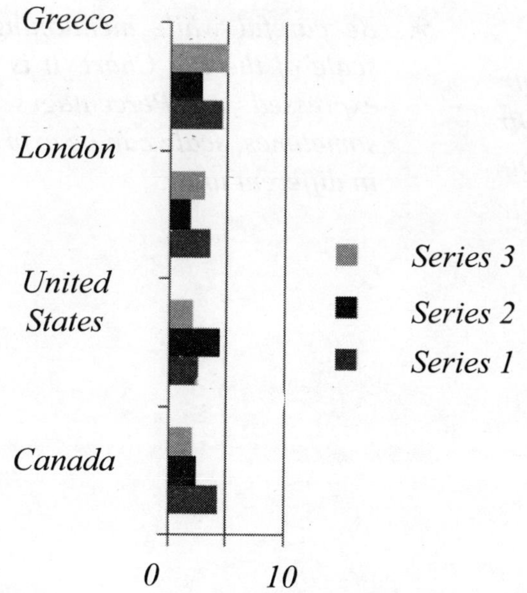

- ✯ *Describe the highest value to the lowest value,*

  Or the lowest value to the highest value
- ✯ *If there are many bars, an individual can sometimes Group Together for description 1 or 2 or 3 bars which have similar or the same values.*
- ✯ *If there are many bars and the individual can't group them, then describe the ones that are the most significant.*

Example (Tips) : Table Representation

Grade/Year	1999	2000	2001	2002	2003	2004
Kindergarten	2.4	2.5	2.6	2.7	2.7	2.8
Grades 1-2	1.5	1.2	1.3	1.5	1.8	2.1
Grades 3-4	1.6	1.7	1.8	1.9	2.1	2.2
Grades 5-6	1.5	1.3	1.3	1.6	2.1	2.6
Grades 7-8	1.6	1.6	1.6	2.2	2.4	2.5

- ✯ *Describe the highest value to the lowest value, Or the lowest value to the highest value*
- ✯ *Describe all the values and sections that are significant to mention.*
- ✯ *Use an appropriate vocabulary of words to describe the graph.*

Example 4 (Tips) : Pie Chart

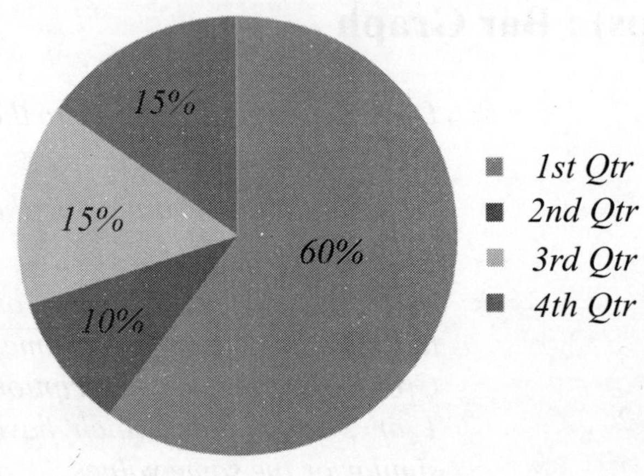

- ✯ *Describe the segments and values.*
- ✯ *Be careful while mentioning the scale of the Pie Chart. It is often expressed in Percentages. But sometimes, scale can be expressed in different units.*

Example 5 (Tips) : Description of The Process

- ✯ *Describe how solar radiation can be utilized to provide domestic hot water and lighting.*
- ✯ *PROCESS: With a process, you must describe how something works or how it is made or used.*
- ✯ *OBJECT: With an object or set of objects, the candidates must describe what something is or what it does. Focus on the relationship between the various parts.*
- ✯ *DATA: With data you, must describe changes, differences or trends. Focus on what these are and why.*

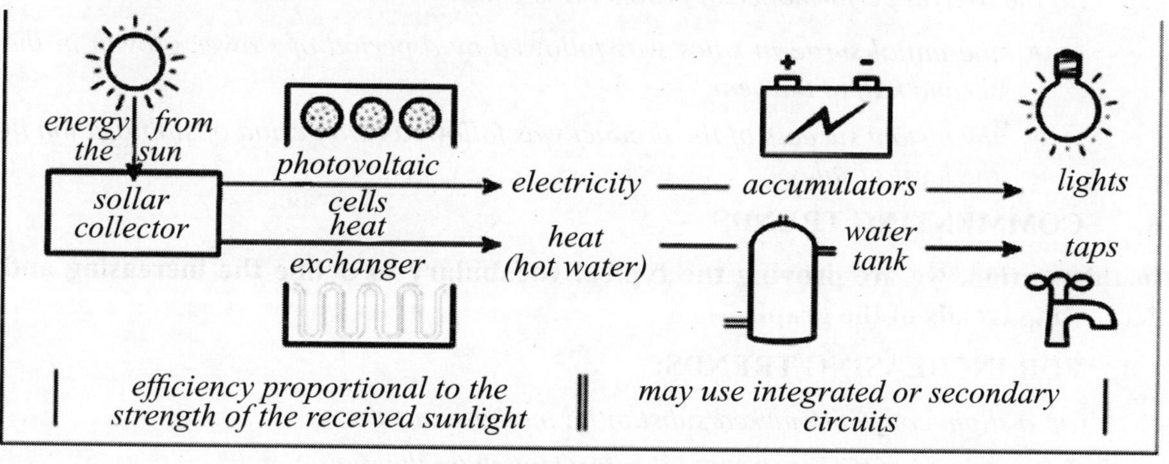

Strategy No. 3 Ready-Made Structure For Writing Task–1

A. PRESENTING VISUALS

(a) *As you will see from this graph......*

(b) *On the line graph, you will note:*

(c) *a strong upward trend in the sales of product A...*

- *despite occasional fluctuations...*
- *with a slight drop during the holiday season ...*
- *with occasional variations due to ...*

(d) *the overall performance of product B is good*

- *the initial surge in sales was followed by a period of slower growth in the second half of the year.*
- *the instant success of the product was followed by a period of stabilization in the level of sales.*

B. COMMENTING TRENDS

In this section, we are proving the typical vocabulary to define the increasing and decreasing trends of the graph.

1. FOR INCREASING TRENDS:

(a) *a slight/constant/marked/substantial increase in sales*

(b) *an increase of about/roughly/approximately/in the region of ...%*

(c) *a little over/above what we predicted- the recovery/upturn began in (month)*

(d) *an overall increase in...*

(e) *an upward trend in the demand for...*

(f) *sales reached record levels/reached a peak in (month)*

(g) *a strong surge in the sales of ...*
by (month) the figure had risen to ...

(h) *we predict that sales will soar in the coming year/over the next ...months.*

2. FOR DECREASING TRENDS:

(a) *just under our target*

(b) *way below our expectations*

(c) *a slight/notable/significant decrease in*

(d) a drop of about ...% in ...

(e) a slight/regular/dramatic decline/reduction in ...

(f) the downturn began in (month)

(g) the situation began to deteriorate in (month)

(h) the number has continued to fall

3. FLUCTUATIONS/VARIATIONS:

(a) a slow start developed into steady progress in sales

(b) an initial upward trend was followed by ...

(c) we note slight fluctuations throughout the year

(d) normal seasonal variations are the cause of occasional downward trends

(e) sales have been (rather) irregular

(f) the level/the rate has been unstable since ...

(g) you will note a certain instability in the rate of ...

C. Conclusions

(a) Appropriate measures must be taken ...

(b) The only option we have is to ...

(c) These changes are inevitable...

(d) The result/outcome will be ...

Strategy No. 4 : Vocabulary For Describing A Graph

Verbs	Nouns	Verbs	Nouns
Rise (to)	A Rise	Reduce (to)	A Reduction (of)
Increase (to)	An Increase		A Slump
Go up (to)			
Grow (to)	Growth	Level out	A Levelling out
Climb (to)	A Climb	No change	No change
Boom	A Boom	Remain stable (at)	
Peak (at)	(Reach) a peak (at)	Remain steady (at)	
Fall (to)	A Fall (of)	Stay(at)	
Decline (to)	A Decline (of)	Stay constant (at)	
Decrease (to)	A Decrease (of)	Maintain the same level	
Dip (to)	A Dip (of)		
Drop (to)	A Drop (of)		
Go Down (to)			
ADJECTIVES	**ADVERBS**	**ADJECTIVES**	**ADVERBS**
Dramatic	Dramatically	Rapid	Rapidly
Sharp	Sharply	Quick	Quickly
Huge	Hugely	Swift	Swiftly
Enormous	Enormously	Sudden	Suddenly
Steep	Steeply	Steady	Steadily
Substantial	Substantially	Gradual	Gradually
Considerable	Considerably	Slow	Slowly
Significant	Significantly		
Marked	Markedly		
Moderate	Moderately		
Slight	Slightly		
Small			
Minimal	Minimally		

WRITING TASK–2

<u>Strategy No. 5 : Structure For Writing Task-2</u>

Magic of Rhetorical Devices

(An Art of Writing English)

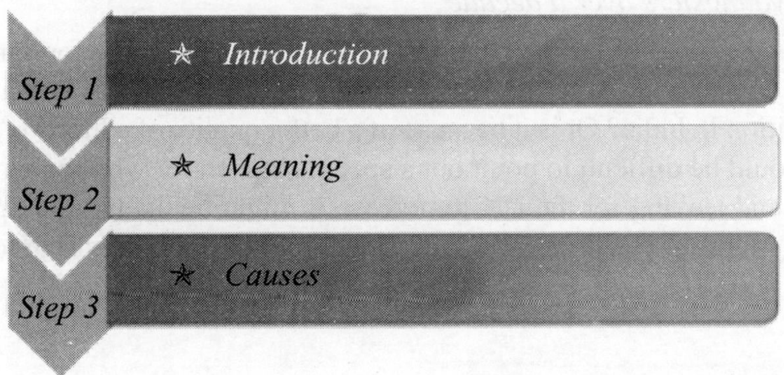

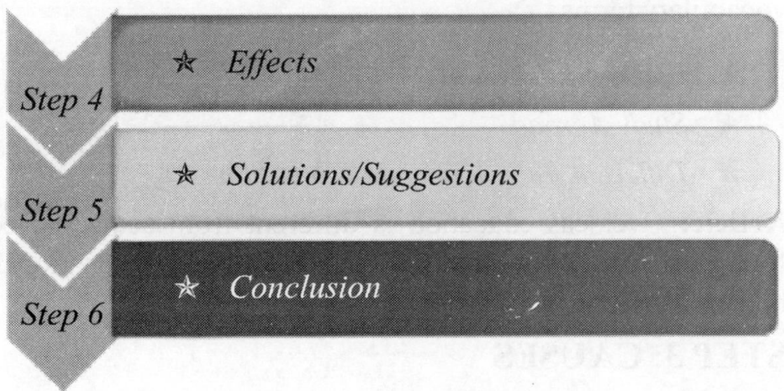

Here, we are providing one an example to illustrate Strategy No. 5

EXAMPLE

Topic: Craze for Overseas Education among Indians

STEP 1: INTRODUCTION

Introduce the topic

- *Overseas Education is the order of the day*
- *Better opportunities of development in abroad*
- *A trend and prestige issue*
- *Craze among Punjabi youngsters over a decade*

Article: Overseas Education is the order of the day. The influx of Indian students to foreign universities and colleges is on the rise. So what propels students to study overseas? Is it because of too much of competition in India? Or is it because of a better quality of education? Or is it a global exposure? It would be difficult to point out a specific reason for why the girl next door is packing her bags and leaving for the UK tomorrow. It might be the frustrating education at system in India; it might be freedom from home; she might even be desiring to add value to her CV.

STEP 2: MEANING

In this step, students are advised to provide the meaning of the topic in their own independent vocabulary terms.

- *Foreign Education*
- *Study Abroad*
- *Different from Academic Education*

Article: Overseas education is different from academic education. In other words, it is foreign education. Foreign universities provide internationally recognized qualifications of higher standards.

STEP 3: CAUSES

In this step, students are advised to provide the logic and reasons behind the topic, which include its positive and negative aspects.

- *Lack of Educational & Job Opportunities*
- *Defective Indian Educational System*

★ *Proper due is not granted.*

Article: Now let's discuss all those reasons why overseas education has today become a craze for the youngsters. It may be due to lack of educational and job opportunities for the Indian Youth, in India, Defective Indian Educational System, Proper Due is Not Granted According to Worth, etc.

3A. POSITIVE

★ *Become a Global player*

★ *Opens up opportunities in international markets*

★ *Adds value to your CV*

★ *Provides environment to acquire skills*

★ *Broadens your horizon*

Article: Moreover, foreign education offers them international exposure, opens up opportunities in international job markets, adds value to your CV, provides environment to acquire skills that you might not learn in a domestic environment, and broadens your horizons. But all these doesn't mean that foreign education does not suffer from defects.

3B. NEGATIVE

★ *Loss of Talented Youth and Caliber*

★ *Problem of Racialism*

★ *Jobs are not According to Their Worth.*

★ *Step-brotherly Treatment*

★ *Too Many Restrictions, Rules and Regulations*

Article: The basic disadvantage of foreign education is the problem of racialism. The recent attacks on Indians and their ill-treatment by foreigners. Everyday Indians are losing their dignity on foreign grounds. Not only this, they are also restricted to so many hard and fast rules which curtail the individual liberty at every step.

STEP 4. EFFECTS (CONSEQUENCES OF THE TOPIC)

In this step, students are advised to highlight the consequence of the topic.

★ *Academic education will lose its gleam*

★ *Talent goes waste*

★ *Disgracing cultural dignity and humanity*

★ *Geniuses of Indians disposed of in just few dollars*

Article: Overseas Education affects Academic Education. It will lose its gleam as most of the talents of India are utilised by foreigners. In this way, the geniusness of Indians is disposed of in no time. Moreover, when indians start doing job there, they are even ready to compromise with their worth and sell their labour in just few dollars. This reflects the cripple attitude of the Indian youth on foreign grounds.

STEP 5 SOLUTIONS

Students are advised to provide solutions to the problems.

- ★ *Provide ample job opportunities to the Indian youth*
- ★ *The government should make some particular strategy*
- ★ *Be patriotic towards your nation*
- ★ *Due according to the worth*

Article: Here the government can step forward and adopt some strategy or policy to save the talent and the caliber of the Indian Youth and provide them ample job opportunities so that they stop even thinking of settling abroad. Moreover, rules and regulations related to Visa Application should be revised.

STEP 6 CONCLUSION

In this step, conclude the topic with certain values, norms and morals.

- ★ *Go abroad just to learn, not to settle.*
- ★ *East or West, India is the best.*
- ★ *Be patriotic.*

Article: At the end, I would like to say that *Overseas Education* is good to learn, but not to settle. One-should not forget that education cannot be received but only achieved with intricate self worth. Then what matters if its an Indian education or foreign education? One should be devoted and dedicated towards one's nation and serve that nation till his/her last breadth.

Strategy No. 6 : 'W' Family

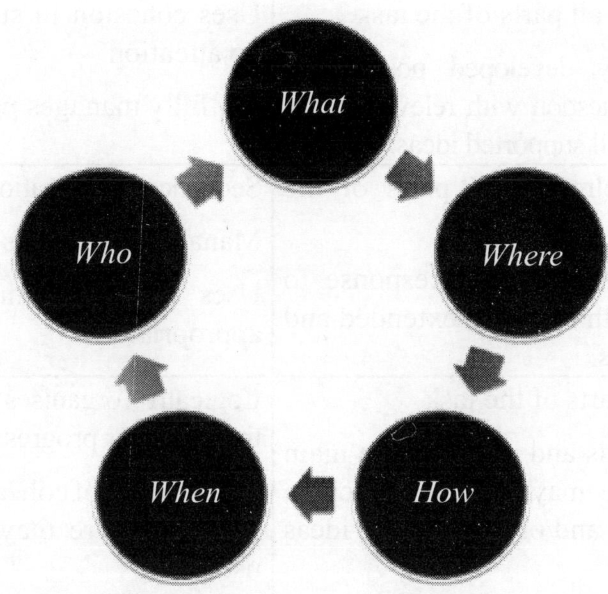

EVALUATION OF 'W' FAMILY

Whenever a candidate wants to write an article, then just before writing think over all the questions related to that topic. Then the next task is just to find the answers to all those interrogations:

TOPIC	CRAZE FOR OVERSEAS EDUCATION AMONG STUDENTS
Why...	Overseas Education?
Who...	Will provide you overseas education?
Where...	People go for overseas education?
What...	Are those reasons because of which Indian students prefer to study abroad?
How...	Can you make your future secure by adopting overseas education?

Band Description

IELTS Task 2: Writing Band Descrption (public version)

Band	Task Response	Coherence & Cohesion
9	Fully addresses all parts of the task. Presents a fully developed position in answer to the question with relevant, fully extended and well supported ideas.	Uses cohesion in such a way that it attracts no attention. Skilfully manages paragraphing.
8	Sufficiently addresses all parts of the task. Presents a well-developed response to the question with relevant, extended and supporting ideas.	Sequences information and ideas logically. Manages all aspects of cohesion well. Uses paragraphing sufficiently and appropriately.
7	Addresses all parts of the task. Presents, extends and supports the main ideas, but there may be a tendency to overgeneralise, and/or supporting ideas may lack focus.	Logically organises information and ideas; there is clear progression throughout. Uses a range of cohesive devices appropriately although there may be some under forever use. Presents a clear central topic within each paragraph.
6	Addresses all parts of the task although some parts may be more fully converted than others. Presents a relevant position although the conclusions may become unclear or repetitive. Presents relevant main ideas, but some may be inadequately developed or unclear.	Arranges information and ideas coherently and there is a clear overall progression. Uses cohesive devices effectively, but cohesion within and or between sentences may be faulty or mechanical. May not always use referencing clearly or appropriately. Uses paragraphing, but not always logically.
5	Addresses the task only partially, the format may be inappropriate in places. Expresses a position, but the development is not always clear.	Presents information with some organisation but there may be a lack of overall progression. Makes inadequate, inaccurate or over emphasising topics/subjects.

Lexical Resource	Grammatical Range and Accuracy
Uses a wide range of vocabulary with very natural and sophisticated control of lexical features; rare minor errors occur only as 'slips'.	Uses a wide range of structures with full felexibility and accuracy; rare minor errors occur only as 'slips'.
Uses a wide range of vocabulary fluently and flexibly to convey precise meanings. Skilfully uses uncommon lexical items but there may be occasional inaccuracies in word choice and collocation. Produces rare errors in spellings and for word formations.	Uses a wide range of structures. The majority of sentences and error-free. Makes only very occasional errors or inappropriates.
Uses a sufficient range of vocabulary to allow some flexibility and precision. Uses less common lexical items with some awareness of style and collocation. May produce occasional errors in word choice, spellings and for word formations.	Uses a variety of complex structures. Produces frequent error-free sentences. Has good control of grammar and punctuation but may make a few errors.
Uses an adequate range of vocabulary for the task. Attempts to use less common vocabulary but with some inaccuracy. makes some errors in spellings and for word formations, but they do not impede communication.	Uses a mix of simple and complex sentence forms. Makes some errors in grammar and punctuation, but they rarely reduce communication.
Uses a limited range of vocabulary, but this is minimally adequate for the task. May make noticeable errors.	Uses only a limited range of structures. Attempts complex sentences but these tend to be less accurate than simple sentences.

ABSTRACT

In this chapter, students will be able to study the solved examples of graphical representation which has been collected from different sources of IELTS previous exams. This section will help the students to crack Task 1 (Graphical Representation) according to the format and vocabulary which is already discussed in the last chapter.

Practice Session for Task 1 is provided in this chapter which includes practice exercises related to bar charts, line graphs, table, processes, pie charts, etc. This session will help the student to master the skills of representing graphs, while cracking the IELTS exams.

SOLVED GRAPHICAL REPRESENTATION FOR WRITING TASK–1

GRAPH NO. 1

The graph below shows the rates of Smoking in Malaysia by men and women. Write a report, discussing the information shown below.

You should write at least 150 words.

Allow yourself 20 minutes for this task.

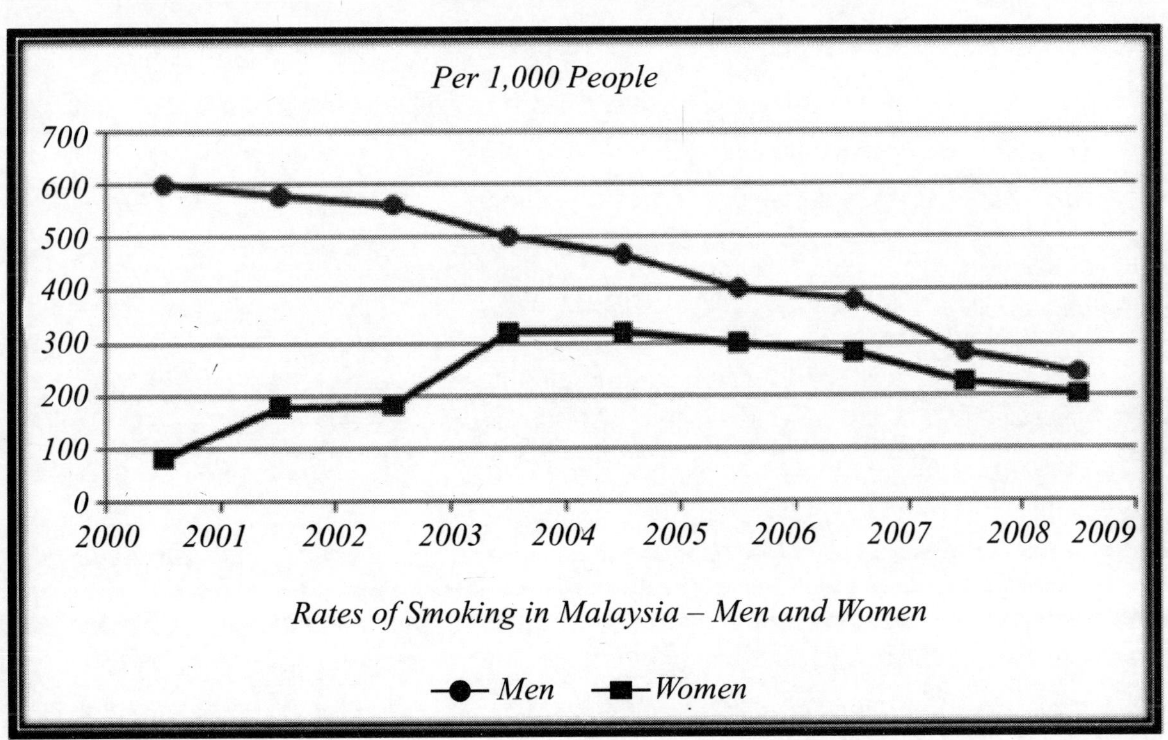

The graph compares the rate of smoking in men and women in Malaysia between the years 2000 and 2009. It can be clearly seen that the rate of smoking for both men and women is currently declining and that fewer women have smoked throughout the period. In 2001, 600 men in every 1,000 were smoking. This number decreased gradually to 500 by 2004 and continued to decrease more steeply to 250 in 2009. In contrast, the rate of smoking in women in 2000 was very low at only 80 in every 1,000. By 2007 this increased to 170, and increased again but more steeply to 320 in 2005. The rate of female smokers then remained stable at 320 until 2006 at which point the figures began to decline and had dropped to 200 by 2000. In conclusion we can see that the rate of smoking in men dropped throughout the whole period but was always at a higher level than the female figures. The rate of smoking in women increased until 2004 but then decreased for the rest of the period.

GRAPH NO. 2

The chart below shows the amount of leisure time enjoyed by men and women of different employment status. Write a report for a university lecturer describing the information shown below.

You should write at least 150 words.

Allow yourself 20 minutes for this task.

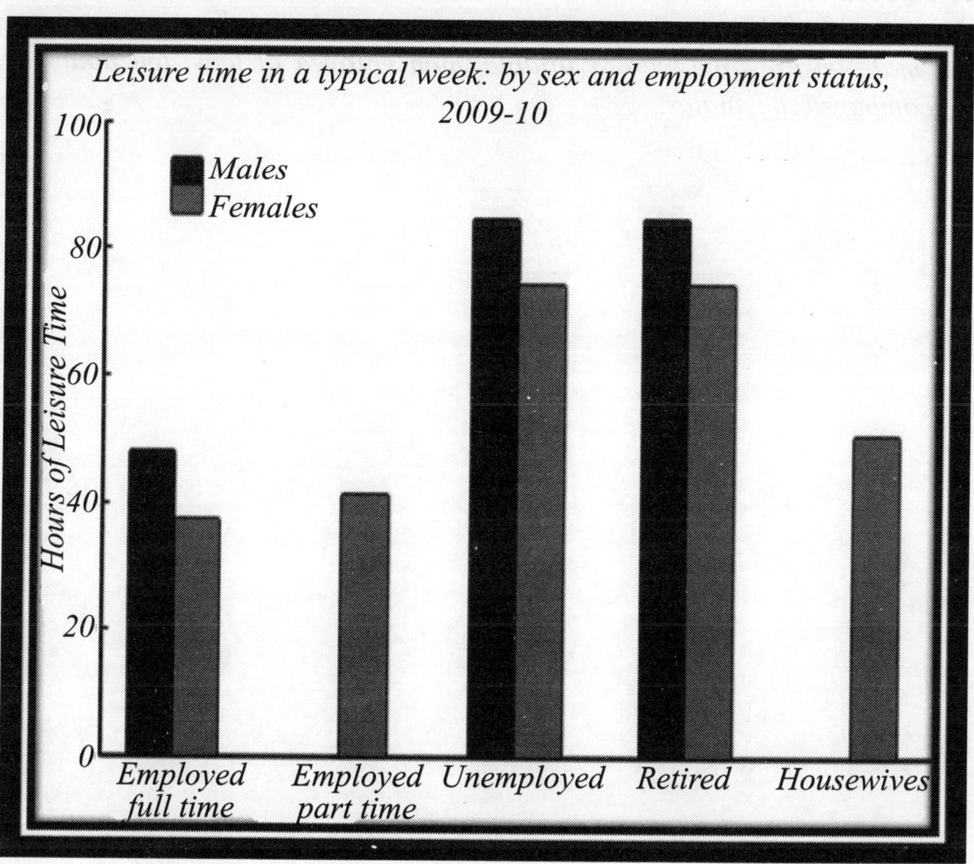

The chart shows the number of hours of leisure enjoyed by men and women in a typical week in 2009-10, according to the gender and employment status. Among those employed full-time, men on average had 50 hours of leisure, whereas women had approximately 37 hours. There were no figures given for male part-time workers, but female part-timers had 40 hours of leisure time, only slightly more than women in full-time employment, perhaps reflecting their work in home. In the unemployed and retired categories, leisure time showed an increase for both sexes, as might have been expected. Here too, men enjoyed more leisure time, over 80 hours, compared to 70 hours for women, perhaps once again reflecting the fact that women spend more time working in the home than men. Lastly, housewives enjoyed approximately 54 hours of leisure, on average. There were no figures given for househusbands! Overall, the chart demonstrates that in the categories for which statistics on male leisure time were available, men enjoyed at least ten hours of extra leisure time compared to females.

GRAPH NO. 3

The diagram below shows the average hours of unpaid work per week done by people in different categories. (Unpaid work refers to such activities as childcare in the home, housework and gardening.)

Describe the information presented below, comparing results for men and women in the categories shown. Suggest reasons for what you see.

You should write at least 150 words.

Allow yourself 20 minutes for this task.

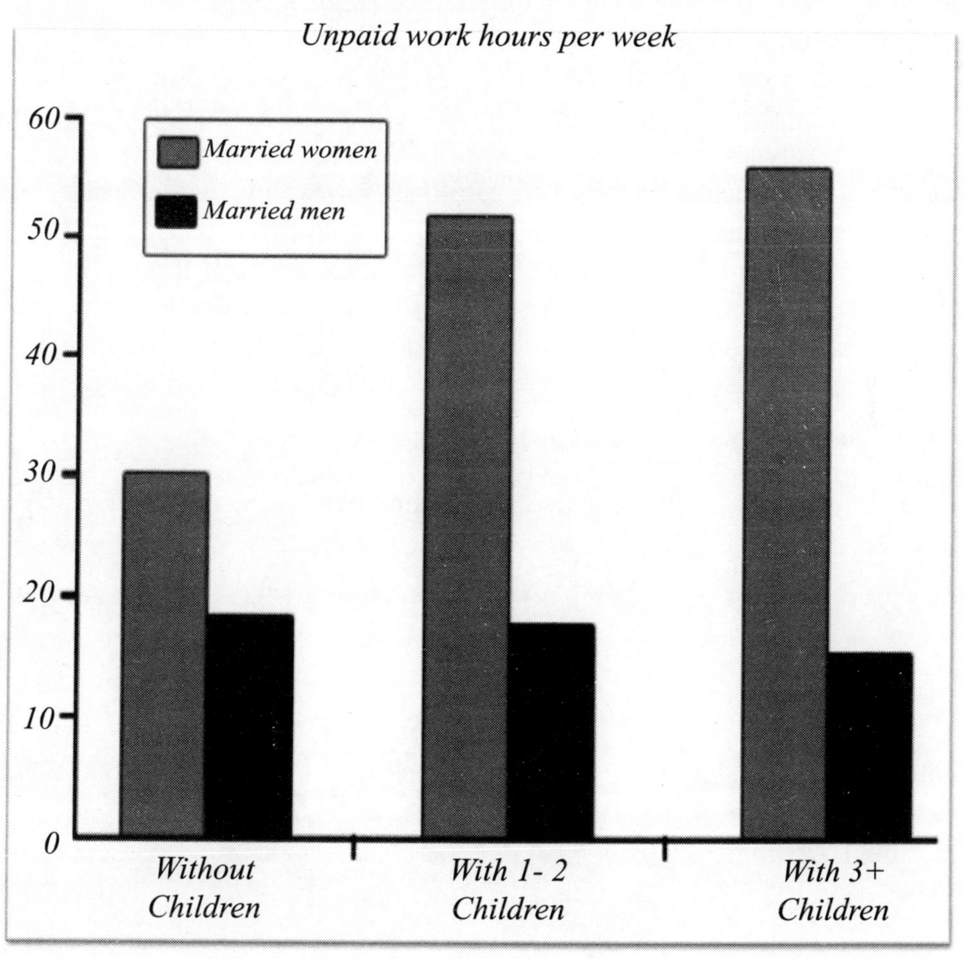

The diagram reveals that the number of hours per week spent in unpaid work is unequally distributed between men and women. In households, where there are no children, women are reported to work some 30 hours per week in such tasks as housework and gardening. Men's contribution to these unpaid jobs averages a considerably lower, (around) 18 hours. When children enter the household, however, the inequality becomes even more pronounced. In families of 1 - 2 children, men maintain approximately the same number of hours of unpaid work as in childless households, but the number of hours women work in the home rises to 52 per week, much of it, no doubt, due to childcare responsibilities.Interestingly, when there are three or more children in the household, men are found to work even fewer hours around the house than before the appearance of the third child. Whereas women's unpaid hours rise to approximately 56 per week, the corresponding figure for men, 16, actually represents a decrease.The data suggests that the increased presence of women in the paid workforce has yet to lead to an increased role for men in their homes.

GRAPH NO. 4

The table below shows social and economic indicators for four countries in 1994, according to the United Nations statistics. Describe the information shown below in your own words. What implications do the indicators have for the countries?

You should write at least 150 words.

Allow yourself 20 minutes for this task.

Indicators	***Canada***	***Japan***	***Peru***	***Zaire***
Annual income per person (in $US)	*11100*	*15760*	*160*	*130*
Life expectancy at birth	*76*	*78*	*51*	*47*
Daily calorie supply per person	*3326*	*2846*	*1927*	*1749*
Adult literacy rate (%)	*99*	*99*	*68*	*34*

A glance at the four indicators of economic and social conditions in four countries, Canada, Japan, Peru and Zaire in 2011 reflects the great differences that exist between the wealthier and poorer nations.The table shows that Japan and Canada had annual incomes of $15 760 and $11 100 per person, respectively. These figures were overwhelmingly greater than the corresponding figures of $160 in Peru and $130 in Zaire. Health indicators, too, reflected overall levels of affluence in the four nations. Life expectancy at birth, for example, was higher among the more economically developed countries. Japan reported the highest life expectancy, 78. This was followed by Canada, 76; Peru, 51; and Zaire, 47. This suggests that richer societies are able to put more money into healthcare than the poorer ones

The amount of calories consumed daily per person roughly followed the same ranking. Each of the Canadians consumed some 3 326 calories per day, while the Japanese took 2846 calories. The corresponding figures for Peru and Zaire were 1927 and 1749, respectively. Literacy rates among adults, too, were higher in wealthier countries, no doubt a reflection of ability to invest in education. Canada and Japan both reported literacy rates of 99%, while Peru claimed 68%. Zaire, the least economically developed of the four countries, had a literacy rate of 34%. The data appear to confirm the often cited link between national wealth, health and educational standards.

GRAPH NO. 5

Eating sweet foods produces acids in the mouth, which can cause tooth decay. (High acid levels are measured by low pH values.) Describe the information below and discuss the implications for dental health.

You should write at least 150 words.

Allow yourself 20 minutes for this task.

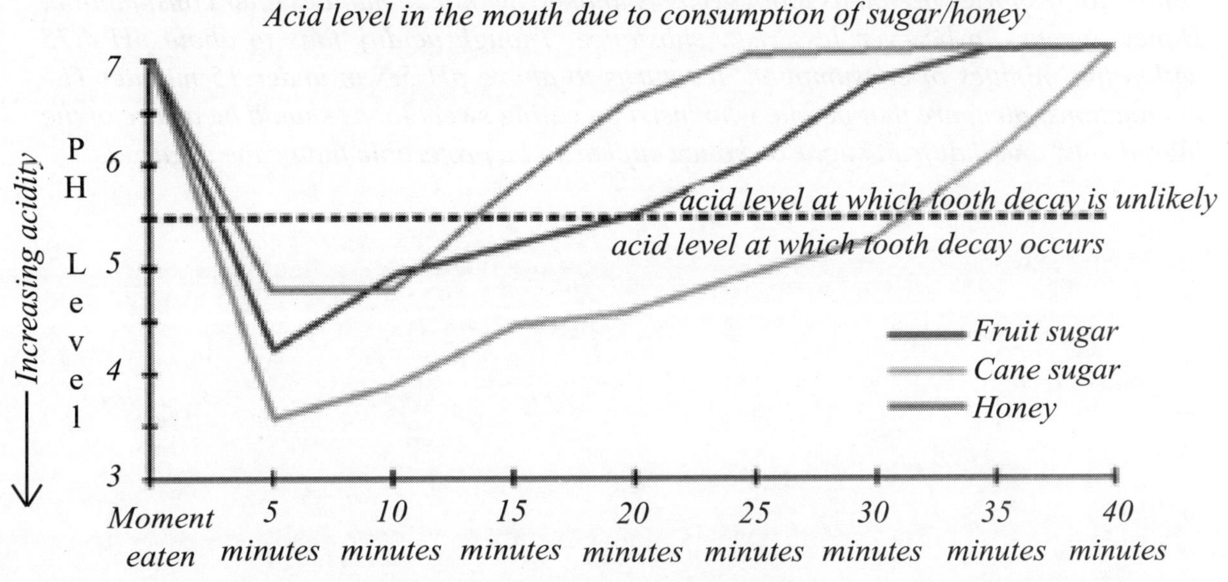

Anyone who has visited a dentist has been told that eating excessive amounts of sweets risks harming the teeth. This is because sweets lower the pH levels in the mouth to dangerous levels. When the pH level in the mouth is kept above 5.5, acidity is such that teeth are unlikely to be in danger of decay. Sweet foods, however, cause the pH in the mouth to drop for a time, and the longer pH levels remain below 5.5, the greater the opportunity for decay to occur. By comparing fruit sugar, cane sugar and honey, which are all common ingredients of sweet foods, we find that cane sugar lowers the pH levels for the longest period, thus producing the greatest risk of the three. Approximately, five minutes after consuming cane sugar, the pH levels drop to as little as pH 3.5. They then begin to rise slowly, but do not rise above the pH 5.5, until at least 30 minutes have elapsed.

By contrast, fruit sugar, which causes the mouth's acidity to fall to just above pH 4, poses a danger for a shorter period as tooth decay is unlikely within 20 minutes after consumption. Honey appears to be even less risky substance. Though acidity falls to about pH 4.75 within five minutes of consumption, it returns to above pH 5.5 in under 15 minutes. The implications, then, are that people who insist on eating sweet foods should be aware of the ingredients, and that fruit sugar or honey appear to be preferable than cane sugar.

GRAPH NO. 6

The graphs below show the numbers of male and female workers in 1995 and 2005 in several employment sectors of Melbourne. Write a report for the university lecturuer describing the information shown.

You should write at least 150 words.

Allow yourself 20 minutes for this task.

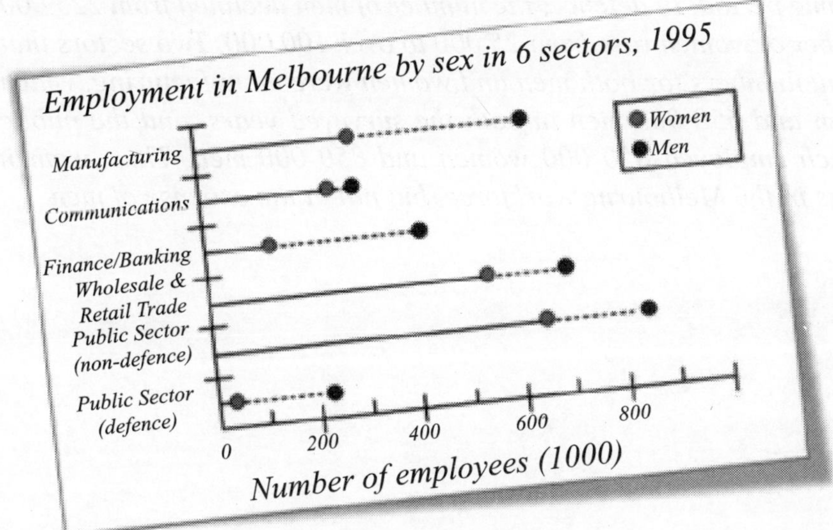

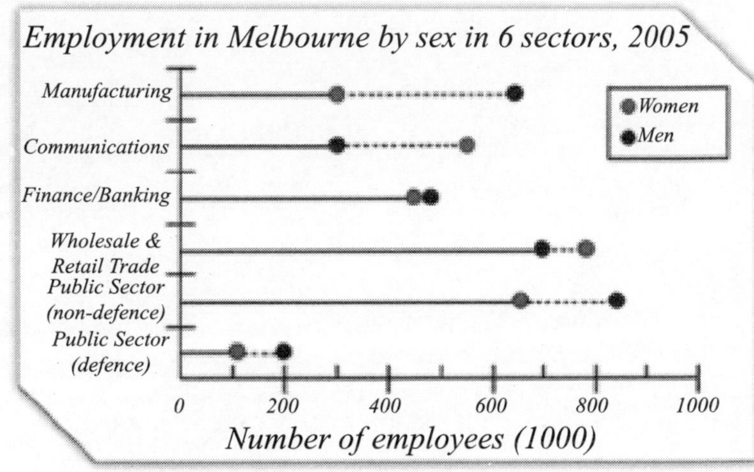

The two decades between 1995 and 2005 brought significant changes in the representation of women in Melbourne workforce, according to the graphs. In 1995, for example, some 300 000 men and 250 000 women worked in the communication sector. Ten years later, though the number of men remained unchanged, the number of women rose to 550 000. A similar situation was seen in the wholesale and retail trade sector, where the number of women rose from about 550 000 in 1995 to almost 800 000, two decades later. The number of men in this sector remained stable over the period, at around 700 000. Women also made gains in both the finance/banking industries and in the defence-related public sector.

Whereas, some 125 000 women worked in finance and banking institutions in 1995, the number increased to 450 000 by 2005. The number of men grew only marginally from 425 000 to 480 000 over the same period. In defence, the number of men declined from 225 000 to 200 000, while the number of women rose from 25 000 to over 100 000. Two sectors that retained stable employment numbers for both men and women were manufacturing, which had about 300 000 women and 650 000 men in both the surveyed years, and the public sector (non-defence), which employed 650 000 women and 850 000 men. Thus, women appear to have made gains in the Melbourne workforce, but not at the expense of men.

GRAPH NO. 7

The graphs below show the types of music albums purchased by people in Britain according to one's sex and age. Write a report describing the information shown below.

You should write at least 150 words.

Allow yourself 20 minutes for this task.

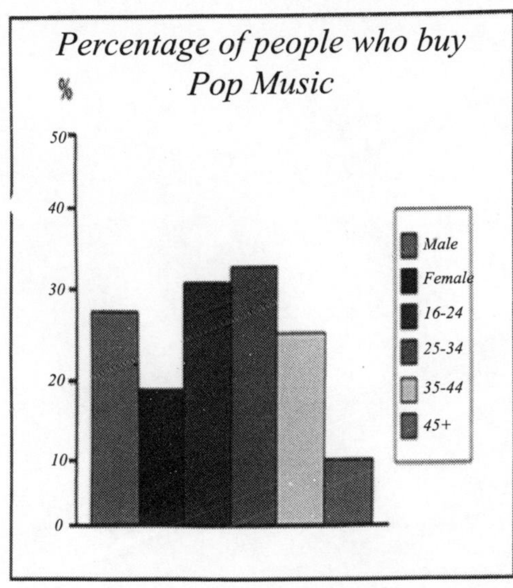

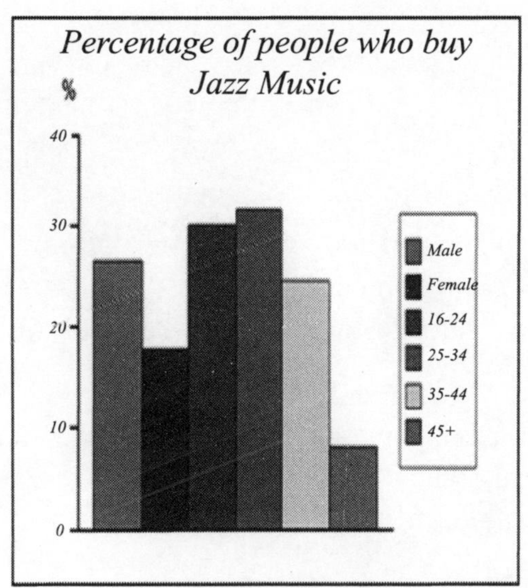

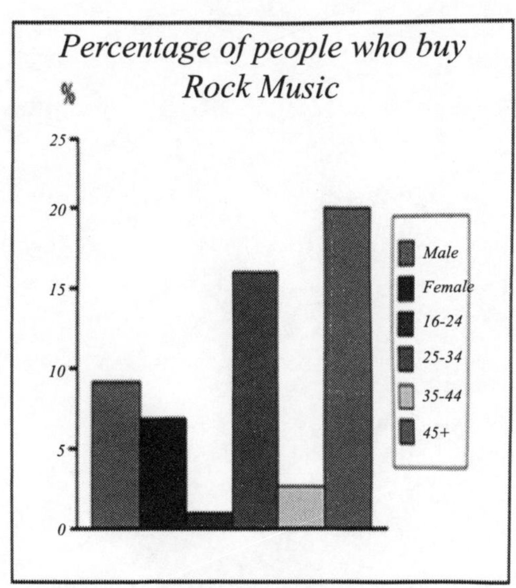

The three bar graphs provide an overview of the types of music people purchase in the UK. At first glance, we see that Rock music is far less popular than Pop or Jazz music. While slightly more women than men buy Pop music. The Jazz market is dominated by men with 30% buying Jazz, compared to 17% of women. From the first graph, we see that interest in Pop music is steady from age 16 to 44 with 20% of the population continuing to buy Pop CDs after the age of 45. The interest in Jazz music reaches its peak among the 25 to 34 year olds, though it never sells as well as Pop. Interest also drops off after the age of 35 with an even sharper fall from age of 45 onwards, a pattern which is the opposite to the Rock music graph.

GRAPH NO. 8

The chart below gives information about global sales of games software, CDs and DVDs or videos. Write a report describing the information.

You should write at least 150 words.

Allow yourself 20 minutes for this task.

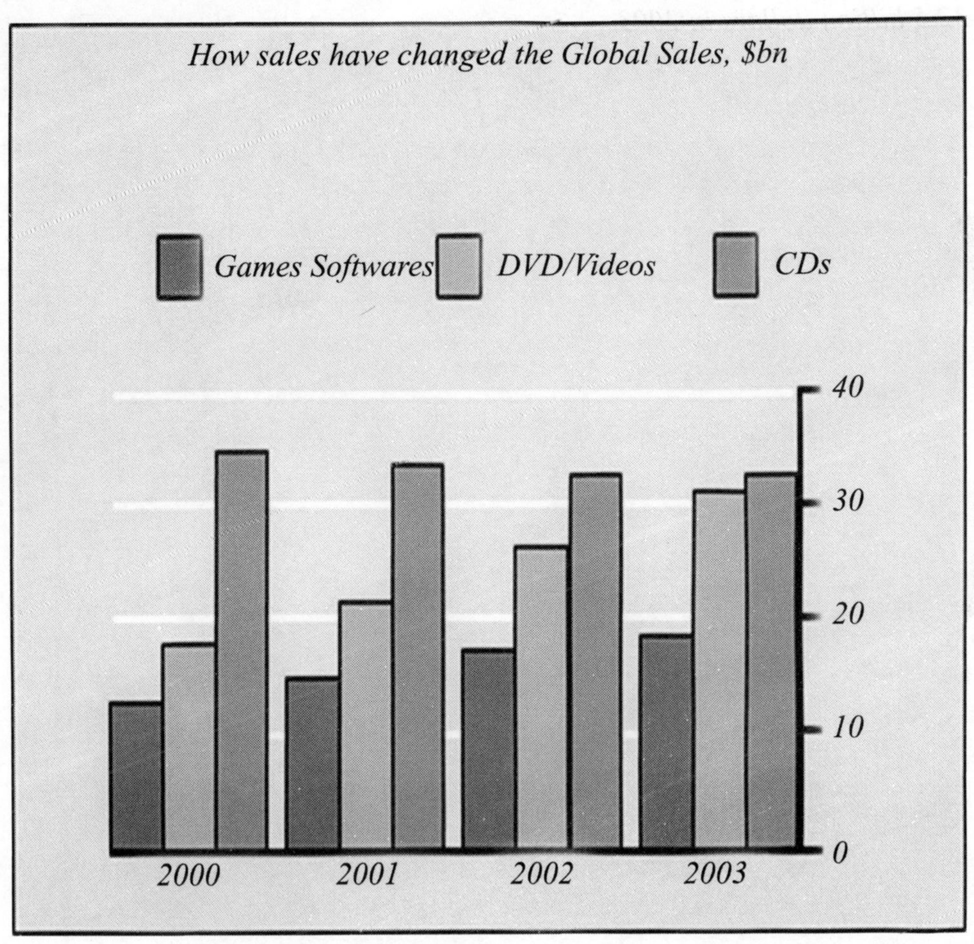

The bar chart shows the changes in the sales of video materials / DVDs, games software and CDs around the world in billions of dollars over a three-year period. It can be seen that the sales of videos / DVDs and games softwares have increased, while the sales of CDs have gone down slightly. Between 2000 and 2003, the sale of videos and DVDs rose by approximately 13 billion dollars. In 2000, just under 20 billion dollars worth of these items were sold, but in 2003, this figure had risen to a little over 30 billion dollars.The sales of games software also rose during this period, but less sharply. Sales increased from about 13 billion dollars in 2000 to just under 20 billion dollars, three years later. On the contrary, during the same time period, the sale of CDs fell from 35 billion dollars in 2000 to about 32.5 billion dollars in 2003.

GRAPH NO. 9

The diagram below shows how a Central Heating System in a house works. Summarise the information by selecting and reporting the main features, and make comparisons where relevant.

You should write at least 150 words.
Allow yourself 20 minutes for this task.

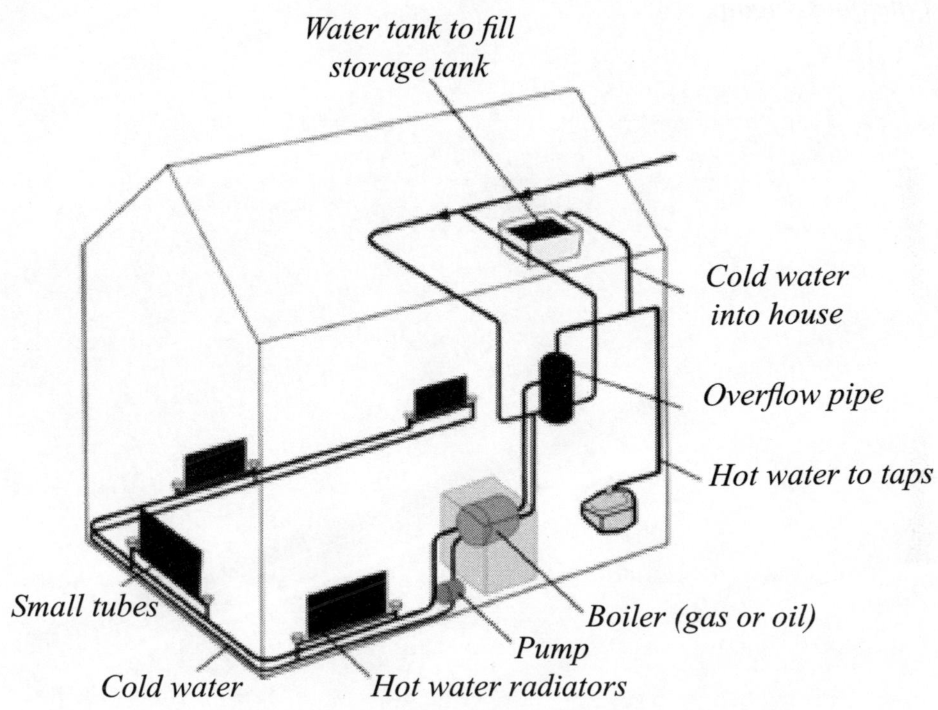

This diagram provides an overview of a domestic Central Heating System. It shows how the tank, boiler and pipes ensure a constant flow of hot water to both the radiators and the taps. The cold water enters the house and is stored in a water storage tank in the roof. From there, it flows down to the boiler, located on the ground floor of the house. The boiler, which is fuelled by gas or oil, heats up the water as it passes through it. The hot water is then pumped a round the house through a system of pipes and flows into the radiators, located in different rooms. The water circulates through the radiators, which have small tubes inside them to help distribute the heat, and this warms each of the rooms. Some of the water is directed to the taps to provide hot water for the house.Once the water has been through the pipes and radiators, it is returned to the boiler to be re-heated and circulated a round the house again.

GRAPH NO. 10

The line graph shows the consumption of renewable energy in Australia from 1975-2000.
Renewable Energy Total Consumption and Major Sources, 1975-2000.

Write a 150-word report identifying the main trends and making comparisons where relevant.

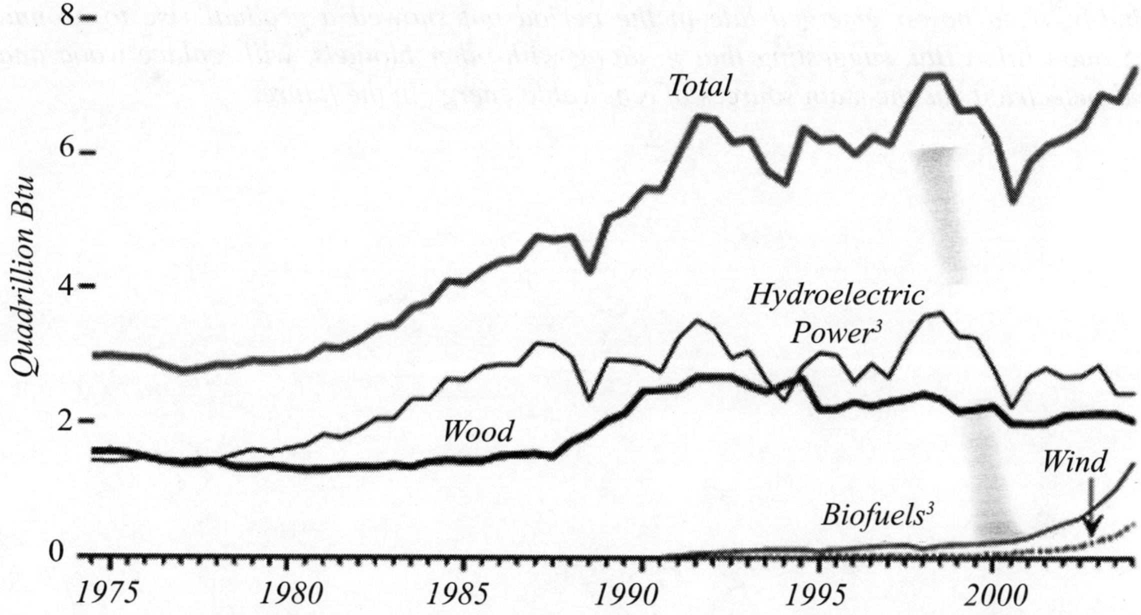

The line graph shows growth in the consumption of renewable energy during the period 1975-2000 in Australia. The results are also broken down by source.

The first thing to note is that the use of renewable energy has doubled over the period, with particularly strong growth in biofuels. This sector did not exist in 1990, but experienced a steep rise during the 2000s to over one quadrillion per year. This made biofuels a serious challenger to both wood and hydroelectric power, which both saw only a limited overall growth. The former grew steadily between 1985 and 1990, but then slipped back to around its original level of 1.8 quadrillion Btu. The later began the period at the same level as wood, but experienced more substantial growth. However, it also fell back to around 2 quadrillion Btu, with a particularly sharp drop in the late 1995.

Finally, wind power emerged late in the period but showed a gradual rise to around 0.5 quadrillion Btu, suggesting that it, along with other biofuels, will replace wood and hydroelectricity as the main sources of renewable energy in the future.

GRAPH NO. 11

The diagram below illustrates the Carbon Cycle in nature.

Write a 150-word description of this diagram for the university lecturer.

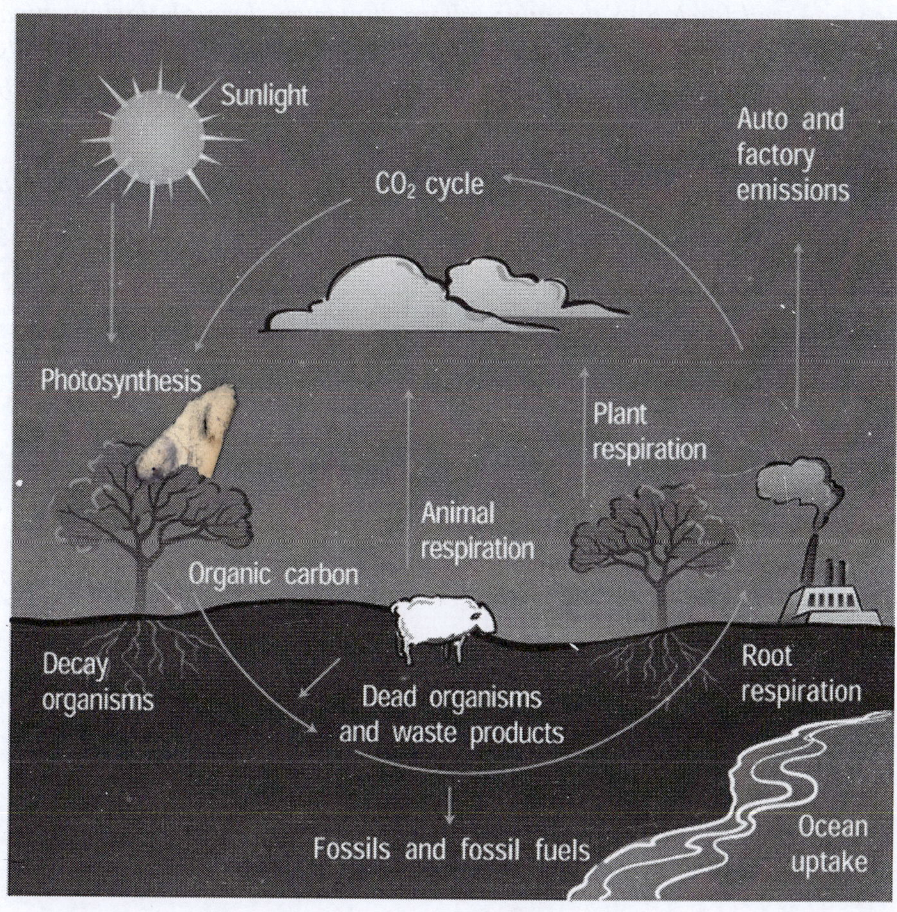

The diagram shows how carbon moves through various stages to form a complete cycle. This report will give a brief description of the main stages in this cycle.

First, we can see that energy from the sun is transformed into organic carbon through a process in plants known as photosynthesis. This organic carbon is then transferred underground when plants and animals that feed on them, die and decay. Some of this carbon is trapped underground in the form of fossils and fossil fuels.

Carbon is also released back into the atmosphere, however, through various means. One is when animals and plants respire, and another is when humans burn fossil fuels in cars and factories. All this carbon enters the atmosphere as CO_2*. It is then reabsorbed by plants and the cycle begins again.*

Overall, we can see that carbon moves in a natural cycle, although human factors may now be affecting the balance.

GRAPH NO. 12

You should spend 20 minutes on this task.

The line graph below gives information about the Sydney Gold Sales.

Write a report describing the information shown. You should write at least 150 words.

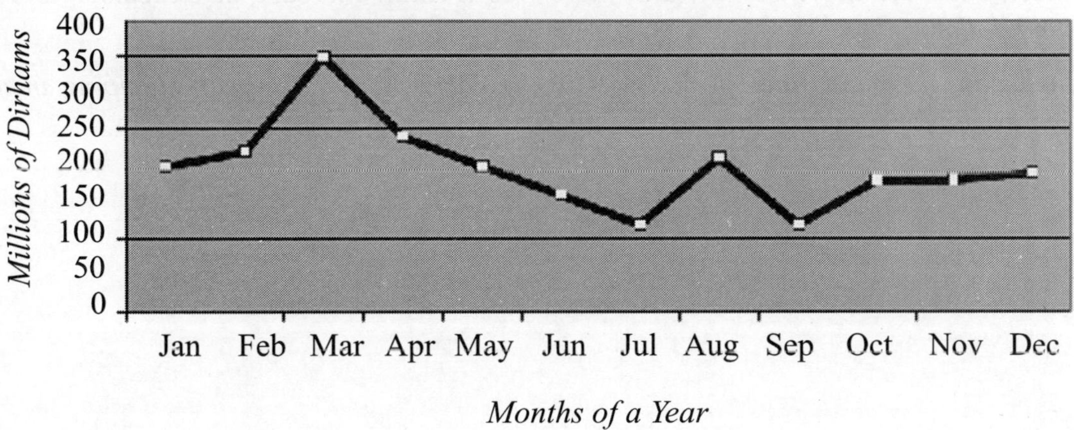

The line graph shows estimated sales of gold in Sydney for 12 months in 2008 in thousands of dollars. There were two main seasons for the gold sales.

The main season for sales is in the December to May period. Sales were consistently above 200 thousand dollars per month, rising sharply to a peak of 350 thousand dollars in March. However, for the next four months, sales declined steadily, reaching an annual low of 120 thousand dollars in July.

In August, there was a sudden increase. Sales almost doubled, rising from 120 thousand dollars in July to 210 thousand dollars in August. This was followed by a drop in September, back to the July figure.

From September to October, sales recovered, from 120 to 180 million. In October and November, sales remained steady, and there was a small increase in December to 190 thousand dollars.

In conclusion, the main sales period was in the early part of the year, slumping in the summer, except for a sudden increase in August.

GRAPH NO. 13

You should spend 20 minutes on this task.

The graph below gives information about how foreign students choose universities for studies in UK.

Write a report for the university lecturer describing the information shown. You should write at least 150 words.

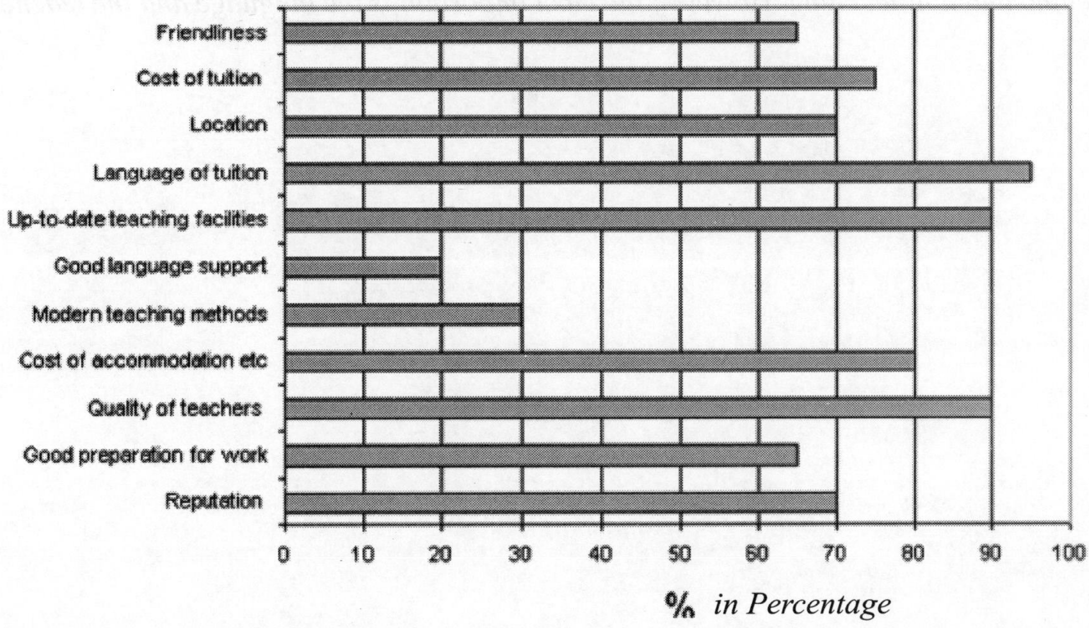

The bar chart shows 11 reasons why the first year students from overseas choose a particular university. The survey of 1,000 first year overseas students was carried out at universities in the UK. The top three reasons are language of tuition, quality of teachers, and up-to-date teaching facilities.

According to the bar graph, the main reason is the language of tuition. At 95% of the sample, it was the main reason most students gave for choosing the university. The second biggest factor was quality of teachers, at 90%, followed by facilities, also at 90%.

Non-teaching factors were also important. Tuition costs were quoted as a reason by 75%, and location was mentioned by 70% of students. The cost of accommodation is also an important factor for 80% of the respondents. Almost two-thirds of students said that the friendliness of the university was also important.

In conclusion, the various factors can be divided into two groups, namely those related to teaching and non-teaching. However, the most important is the language and the teachers.

GRAPH NO. 14

You should spend 20 minutes on this task. The bar chart below shows leisure activities of Australian kids (boys and girls) in all the 8 days what they are doing. Write a report, decreasing the information shown. You should write 150 words.

What kids are doing

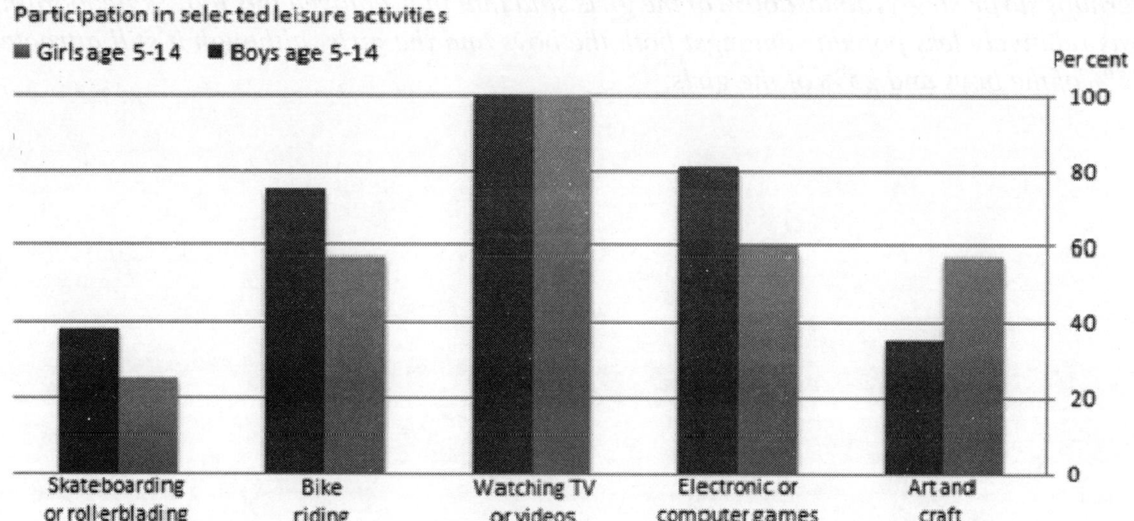

The above bar graph shows the preferred leisure activities of Australian children aged 5-14. As might be expected, it is clear from the data that sedentary pursuits are far more popular nowadays than active ones.

Sedentary 10,000 children that were interviewed, all the boys and girls stated that they enjoyed watching TV or videos in their spare time. In addition, the second most popular activity, attracting 80% of boys and 60% of girls, was playing electronic or computer games. While girls rated activities, such as art and craft – just under 60% stated that they enjoyed these in their spare time. Only 35% of the boys opted for creative pastimes. Bike riding, on the other hand, was almost as popular as electronic games amongst boys and, perhaps surprisingly, almost 60% of the girls said that they enjoyed this too. Skateboarding was relatively less popular amongst both the boys and the girls, although it still attracted 35% of the boys and 25% of the girls.

PRACTICE SESSION (ACADEMIC) FOR WRITING TASK – 1

PRACTICE TEST – 1

The two graphs show the main sources of energy in Australia in 2000 and 2010.Write a report for the university lecturer describing the changes which occurred.

You should write at least 150 words.

Allow yourself 20 minutes for this task.

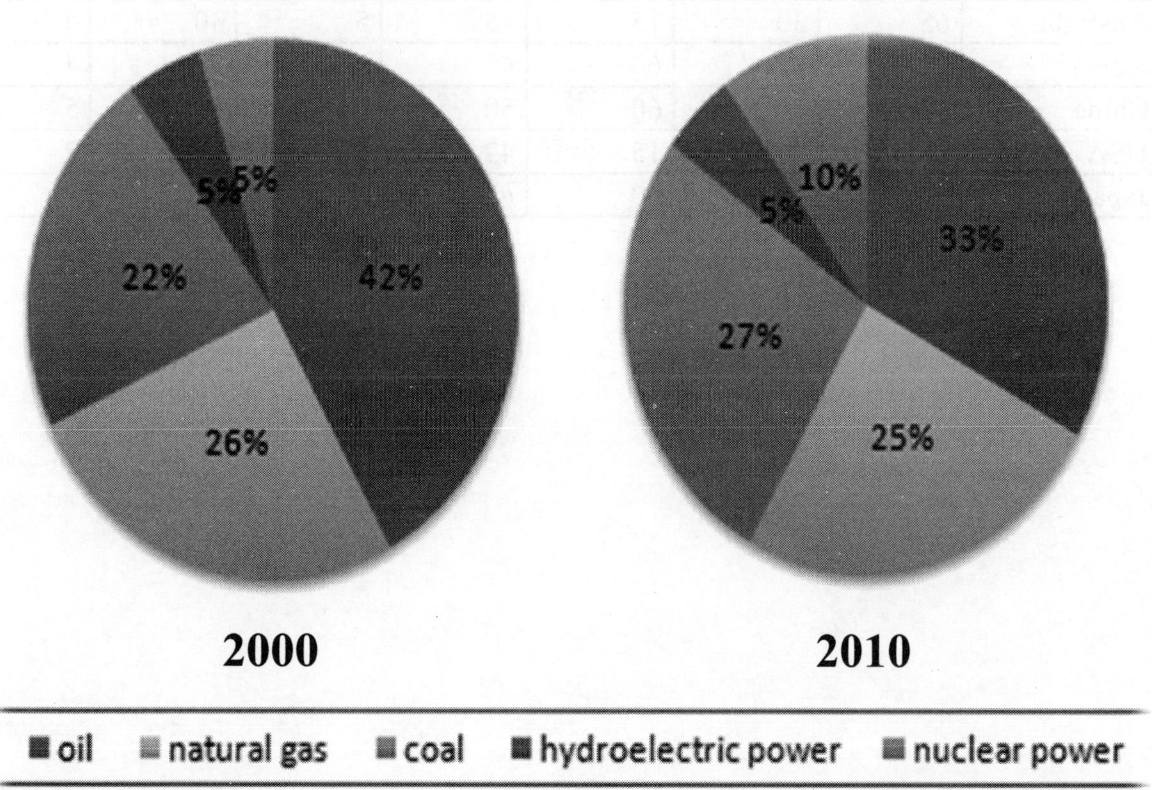

PRACTICE TEST – 2

The table below gives information about Favourite Pastimes in different cities.

Summarise the information by selecting and reporting the main features, and make comparisons where relevant.

You should write at least 150 words.

Allow yourself 20 minutes for this task.

	From 30 - 50 years old						
	TV	Sport	Reading	Hobbies	Music	Beach	Sleep
UK	60	22	15	40	3	0	2
Switzerland	/	/	30	20	4	/	/
India	/	/	30	21	4	/	20
Australia	65	30	15	45	5	30	4
Korea	22	21	60	45	2	2	4
China	15	25	60	50	0	5	5
USA	60	23	15	42	23	30	2
Japan	/	/	60	/	/	/	/

PRACTICE TEST – 3

Write a report for the university lecturer describing the information shown below.

You should write at least 150 words.

Allow yourself 20 minutes for this task.

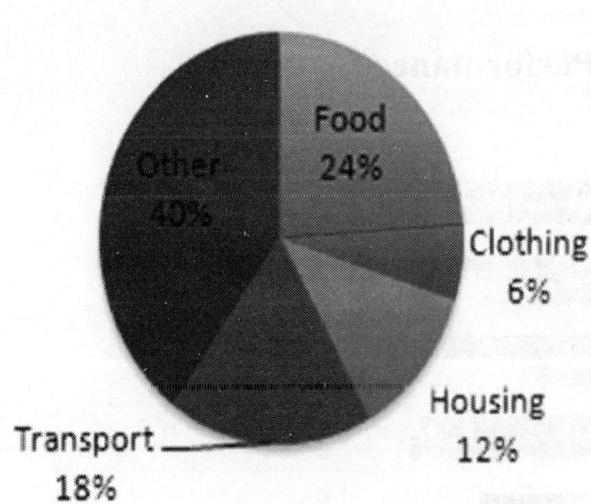

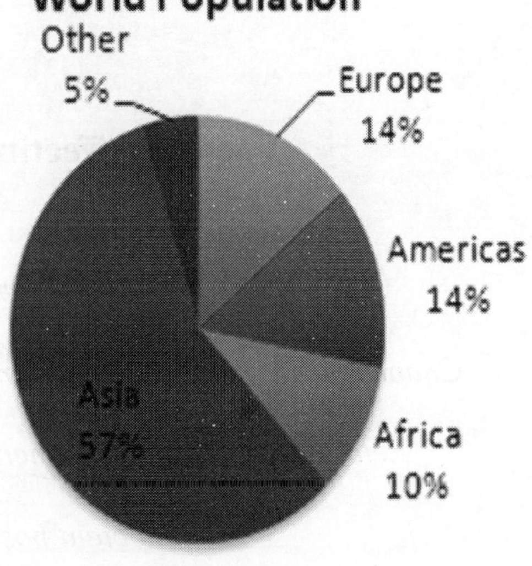

Consumption of Resources

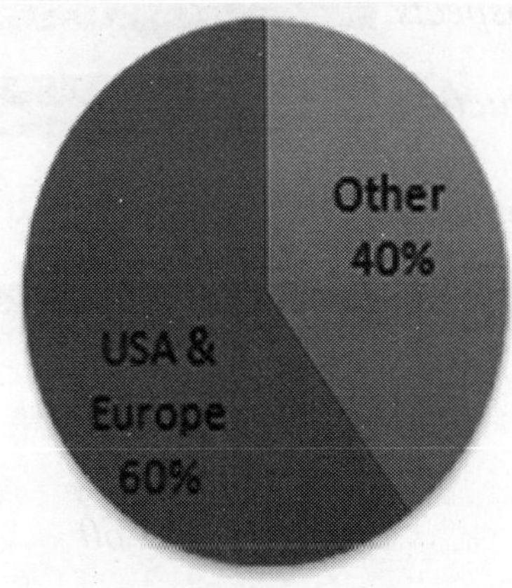

PRACTICE TEST – 4

The bar chart below shows the results of a survey conducted by a personnel department at a major company. The survey was carried out on two groups of workers: those aged from 18-30 and those aged 45-60, and shows factors affecting their work performance. Write a report describing the information shown below.

You should write at least 150 words.

Allow yourself 20 minutes for this task.

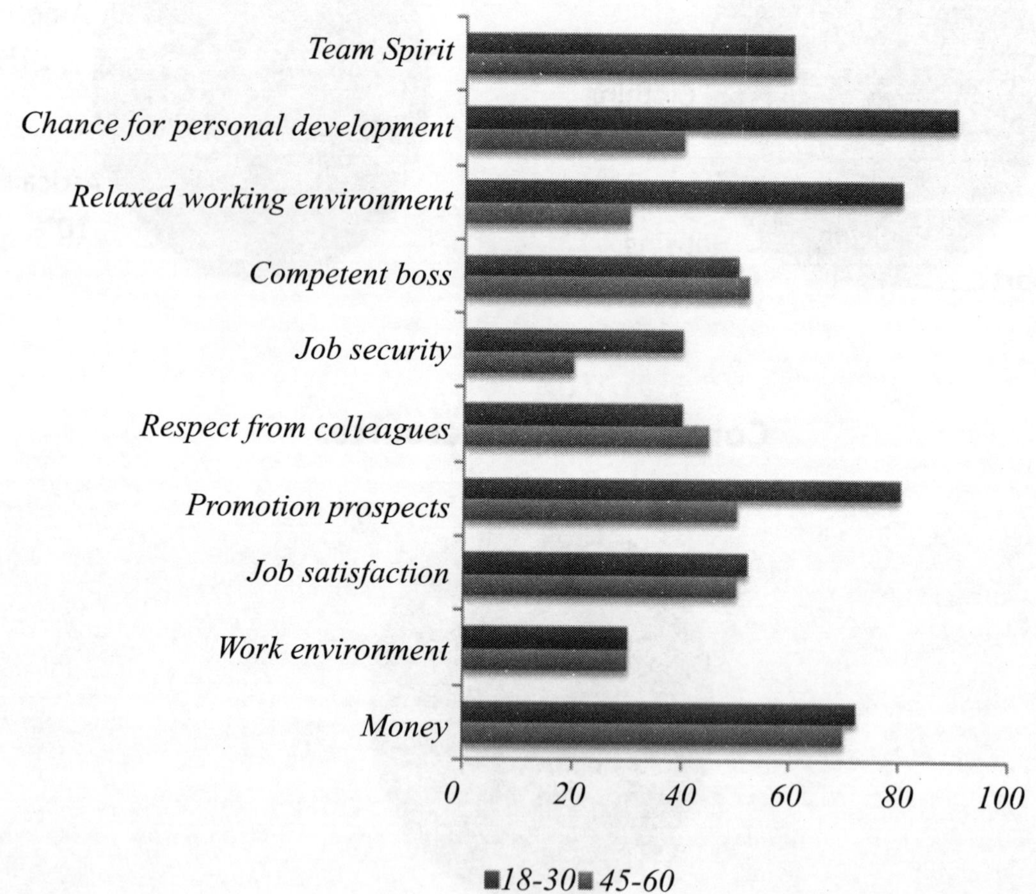

PRACTICE TEST – 5

The chart below shows the estimated world literacy rates by region and by gender for the year, 2000. Write a report for describing the information below.

You should write at least 150 words.

Allow yourself 20 minutes for this task.

Estimated World Literacy Rates, by Region and by Gender, 2000

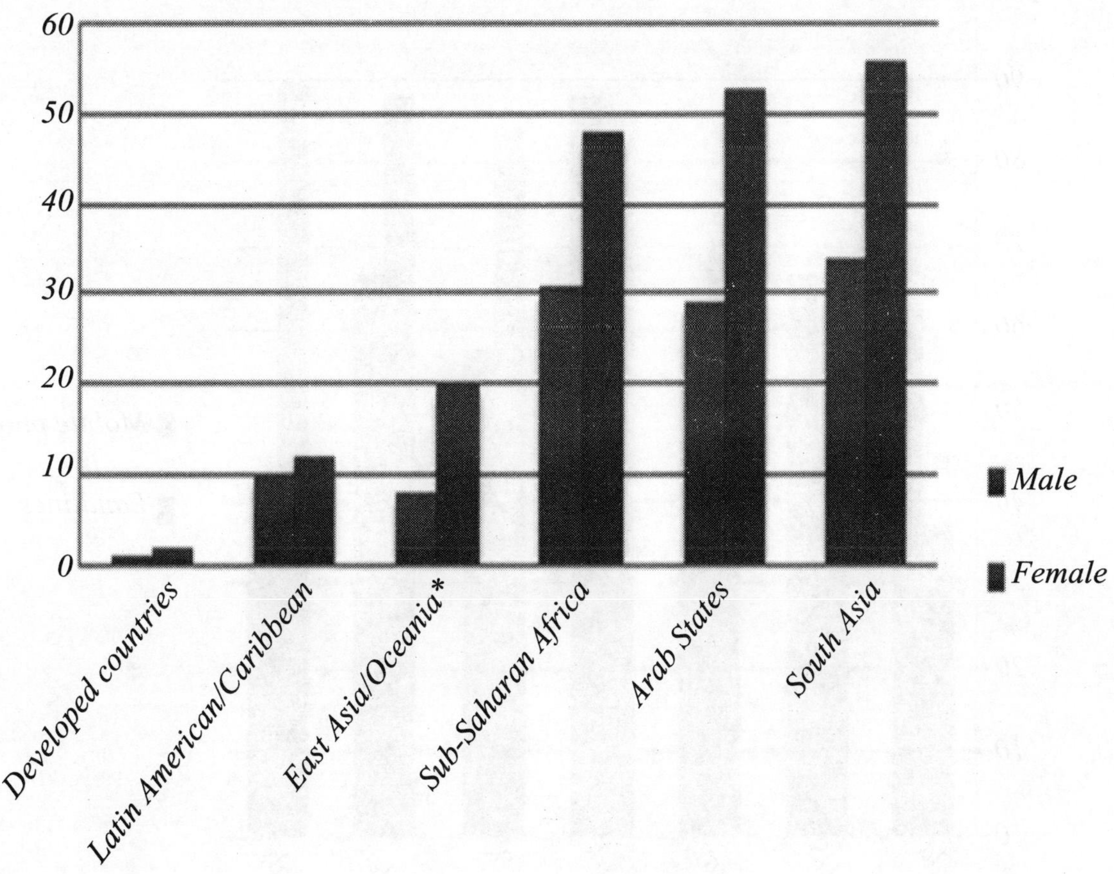

PRACTICE TEST – 6

The chart shows the number of mobile phones and landlines per 100 people in selected countries. Write a report describing the information given.

You should write at least 150 words.

Allow yourself 20 minutes for this task.

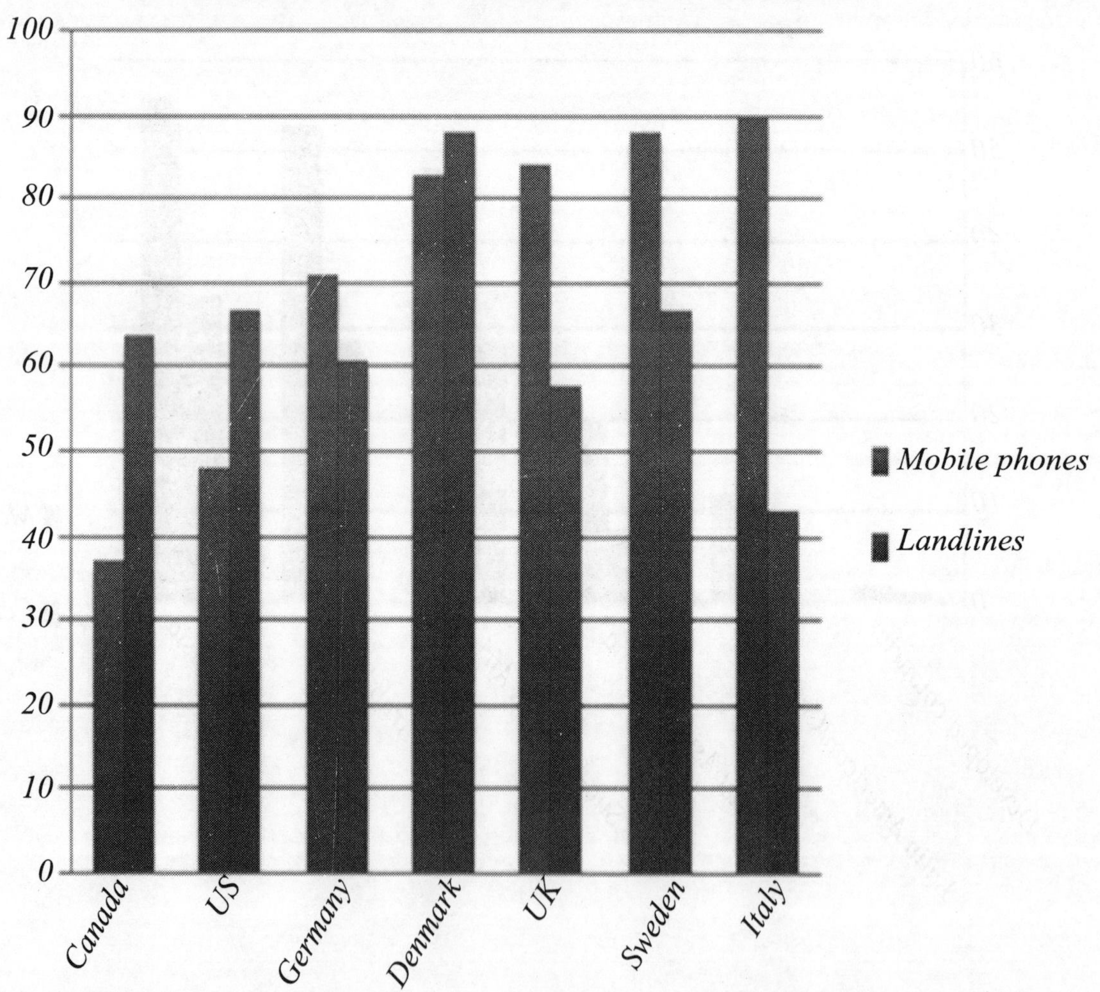

PRACTICE TEST – 7

The graph above show information of employment rates across 6 countries in 2005 and 2010. Summarize the information by choosing and describe the main idea, making comparisons where appropriate.

You should write at least 150 words.

Allow yourself 20 minutes for this task.

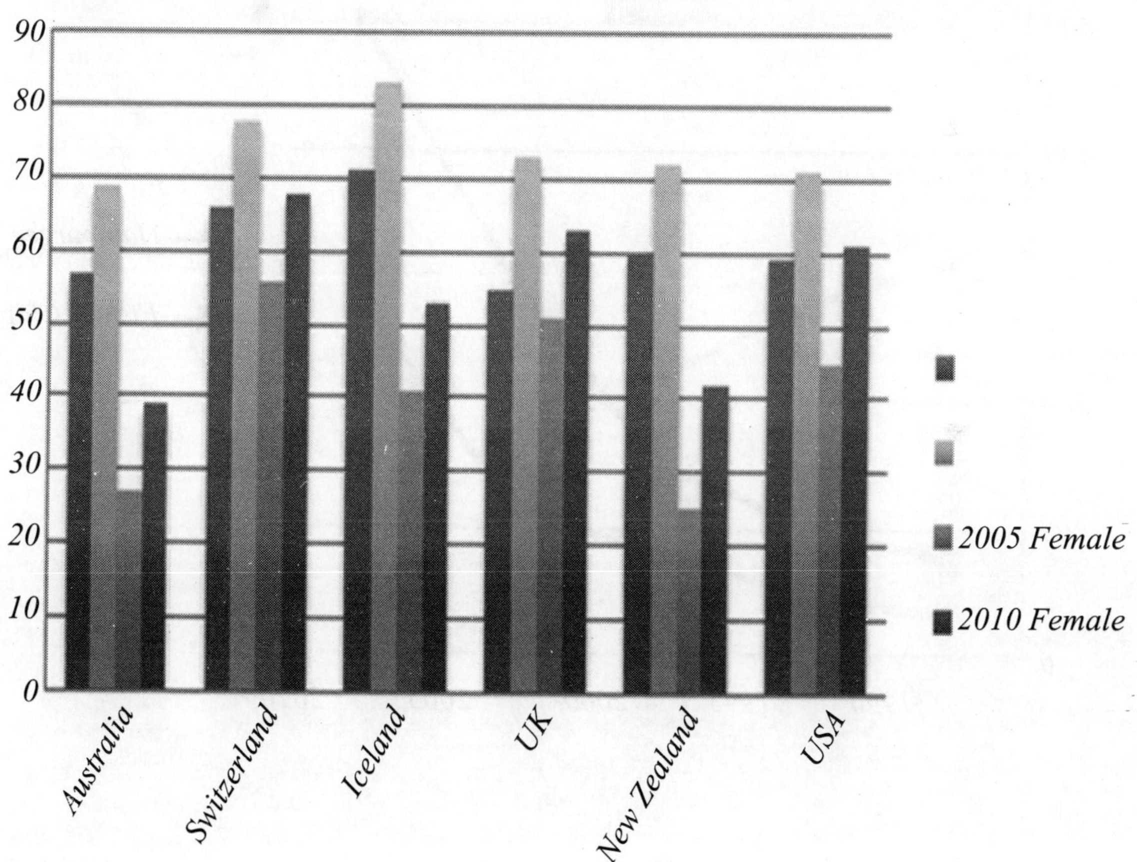

PRACTICE TEST – 8

Write a report for the university lecturer describing the information below.

You should write at least 150 words.

Allow yourself 20 minutes for this task.

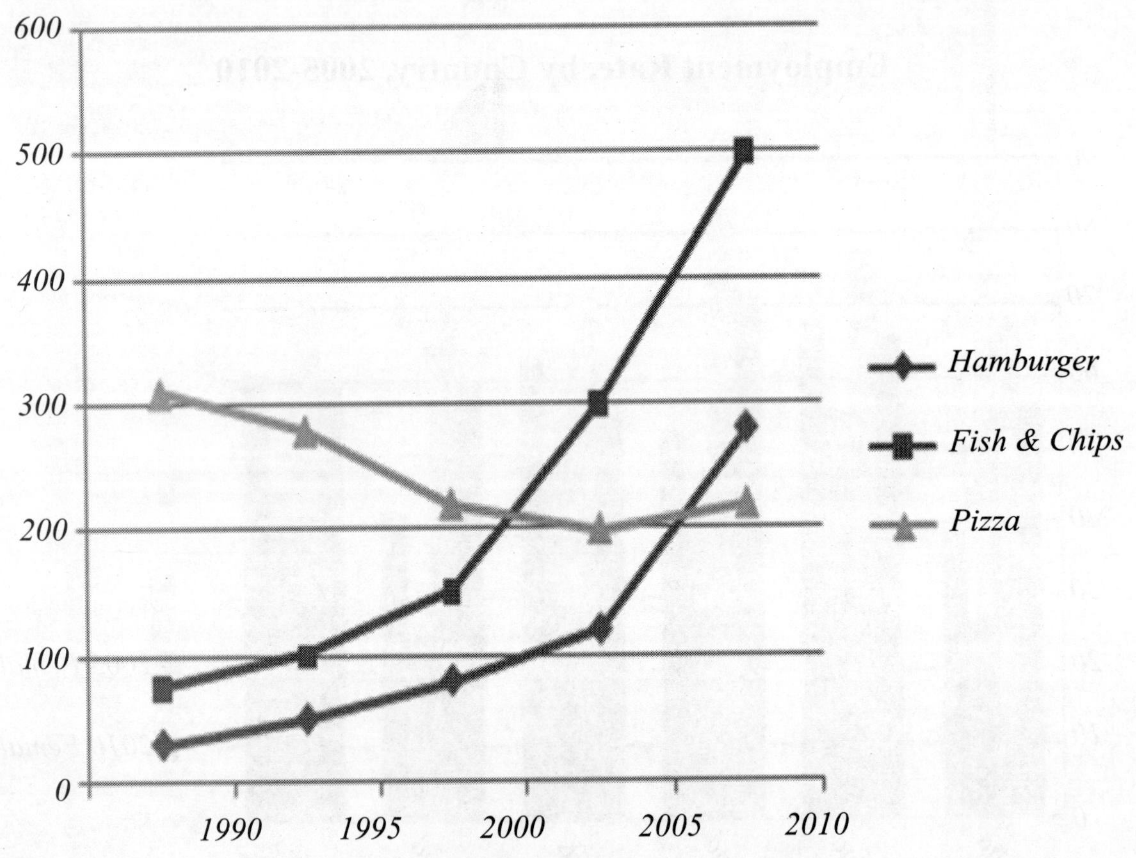

PRACTICE TEST – 9

Write a report describing the Information below.
You should write at least 150 words.
Allow yourself 20 minutes for this task.

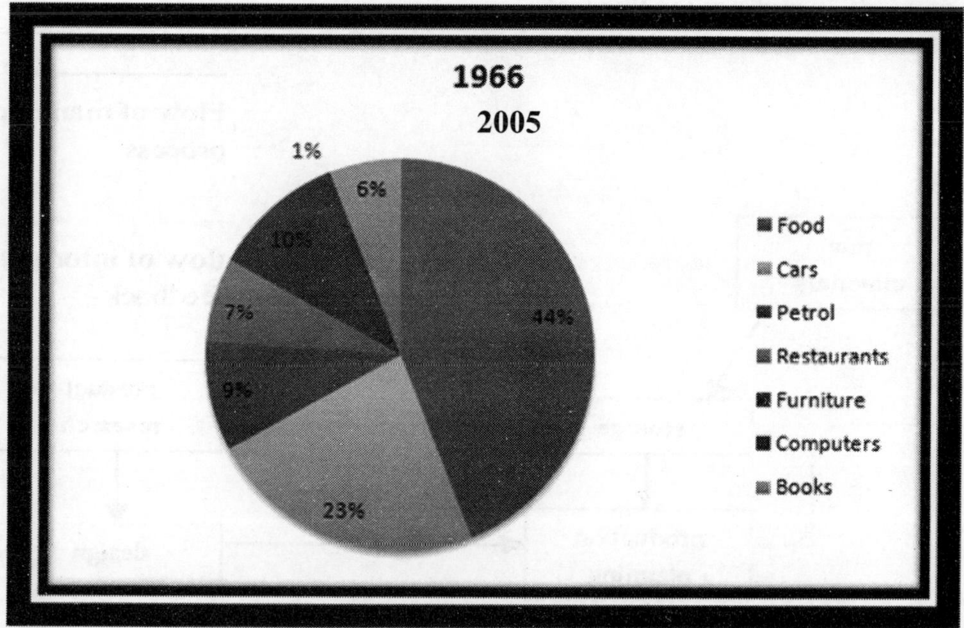

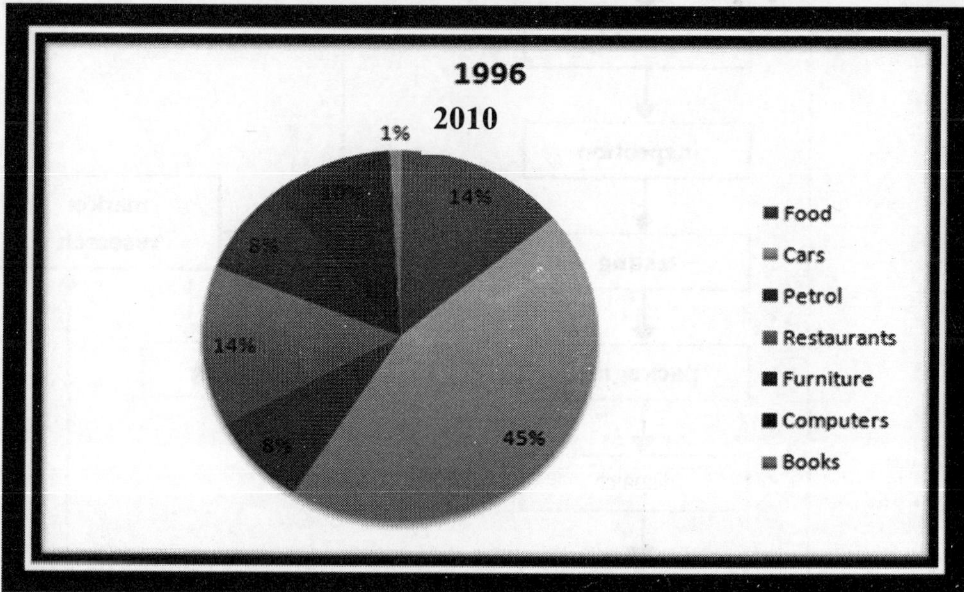

PRACTICE TEST – 10

The diagram below shows the typical stages of consumer goods manufacturing, including the process by which information is fed back to earlier stages to enable adjustments. Describe the process shown below.

You should write at least 150 words.

Allow yourself 20 minutes for this task.

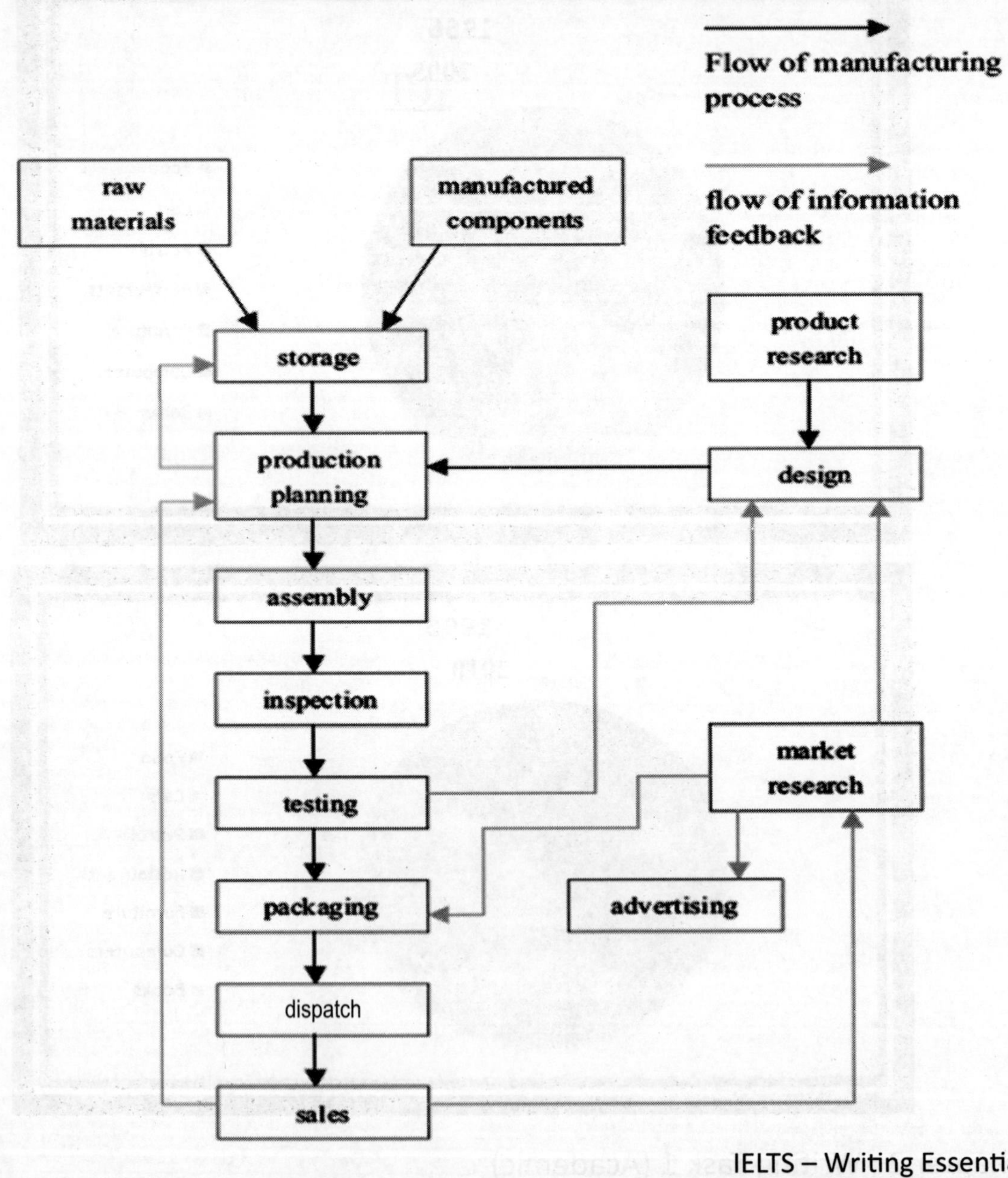

ABSTRACT

The IELTS exam is divided into two categories, one for General and the other for Academic Candidates. For General Candidates, the IELTS demands Letter Writing Skills. To satisfy the General Candidate, we are providing some letters for improving their skills for Task – 1 of the General Candidates. Before some solutions related to letters, we are notifying here certain tips which should be followed and kept in mind while writing a letter.

WRITING TASK – 1
(STRATEGIES)

In the IELTS General Training Writing Test Task 1, the scope of the task is fairly limited. You can practise extremely similar tasks, which will greatly prepare you for the exam.

IELTS Writing Tips :

The IELTS General Training Task 1 Writing Test

The IELTS General Training Writing Test lasts for 1 hour and includes 2 tasks. Task 1 is a letter and you must write at least 150 words. You should spend about 20 minutes out of the hour for Task 1.

The Task for the IELTS General Training Task 1 Writing

The IELTS General Training Writing Task 1 asks you to write a letter of a minimum of 150 words in response to some situation or problem. The task will probably ask you to complain about something, to request information, ask for help, to make arrangements and/or explain a situation. All these are fairly similar tasks.

Marking for the IELTS General Training Task 1 Writing

The IELTS General Training Task 1 Writing will be marked in four areas. You will get a mark from 1 to 9 on *Task Achievement, Coherence & Cohesion, Lexical Resource and Grammatical Range and Accuracy*. Your final band for Task 1 will be effectively an average of the four marks awarded in these areas. Task 1 writing is less important than Task 2 and to calculate the final writing marks, more weight is assigned to the Task 2 mark than to Task 1's mark. To get a good overall marks for The IELTS General Training Writing, though, both the tasks have to be well answered, don't hold back on Task 1 or give yourself too little time to answer it properly. The marking system below can also be used for marking IELTS Practice Tests and it is used to grade the example writing in our the IELTS Practice Tests.

1. **Task Achievement:** This is where you can really make a difference through careful preparation. This mark grades you on basically "have you answered the question". It marks whether you have covered all requirements of the task suffciently and whether you presented, highlighted and illustrated the key points appropriately.

2. **Coherence and Cohesion:** These two are interrelated which is why they are done together. Cohesion is how your writing fits together. Does your writing with its ideas and content flow logically? Coherence is how you are making yourself understood and whether the reader of your writing understands what you are saying. An example of bad coherence and cohesion would be as follows:

1. We went to the beach because it was raining.

Probably the writer of this sentence does not mean "because" as people don't usually go to the beach when it is raining. The writer should have written:

2. We went to the beach although it was raining.

Sentence 1 has made a cohesion and coherence error (as well as a vocabulary one). "Because" does not join the ideas of the sentence together correctly and, as a result, the reader does not understand what the writer wants to say. This is an exaggerated example but it shows what I mean. Good cohesion and coherence is not noticeable as it allows the writing to be read easily. Good cohesion and coherence also includes good and appropriate paragraph usage.

3. **Lexical Resource:** This area looks at the your choice of words. The marker will look at whether the right words are used and whether they are used at the right time in the right place and in the right way. To get a good marks here, the word choice should not only be accurate but wide ranging, natural and sophisticated.

4. **Grammatical Range and Accuracy:** Here the examiner will mark your appropriate, flexible and accurate use of grammatical structures. Many people are worried about their grammar but, as you can see, grammar is only one section of the four used to grade your writing. IELTS is much more interested in communication rather than grammatical accuracy. It is, of course, still a part of the marking scheme and important, as such.

Tips for Wirting Task 1

1. Answering the question

Task achievement (answering the question) is one quarter of your total marks and it is an area in which everyone should do well. This is often, however, not the case.

What you must do is to write a letter, which would fully answer the needs of the problem in a real life situation. Even if you have covered all that the question itself asks, have you included everything in the letter needed to realistically perform its function? For example, a question I have seen somewhere gives the candidate the following task:

You have some library books that you are unable to return, as a member of your family in another city has fallen ill and you have had to go and look after him/her.

Write a letter to the library explaining the situation. Apologize for the inconvenience called and say what you are going to do.

You should write at least 150 words.

This seems a fairly typical IELTS General Training Task 1 writing question. Answering the question in a way that will get you a good Task Fulfilment grade needs a number of things for you to do.

1. Write at least 150 words.

Writing less does not answer the question, which tells you to write at least 150 words. If you write less than 150 words, the examiner marking your paper will give you a maximum of 5 for Task Achievement or even less. Making sure that you write enough is one of the vital things you can do when using the IELTS Practice Tests.

2. Fully do all the things that the question asks you.

In this case, it asks you to do 3 main things:

1. Explain the situation
2. Apologize for the inconvenience
3. Say what you are going to do

The important part is to fully do these things. Don't take one line to explain about your relative – people who do this often don't make the 150 word limit. Enlarge on what the question tells you. Use your imagination. It must be something fairly serious to make you leave town and you must be the only one possible to look after the relative, so go into these things. Be realistic as well.

You're writing to a library and you won't make it too personal. Apologizing won't take up much space, but you can still devote a couple of sentences to it. Saying what you are going to do should be a full explanation as well.

3. Make your letter realistic so it would function in a real life situation.

This involves adding other things to the letter, which it may not ask you for, but without which your letter would not perform its function. For this question, it would mean introducing yourself by name, giving your library card membership number, telling the library the titles of the books that you have borrowed, the names of their authors, their library reference numbers, when you borrowed them and when they were due back.

Finally, in this question, the situation might involve you getting a fine for the late books. So, you could ask politely for that to be cancelled due to the circumstances. Without this information, the letter wouldn't help the library much in real life and, even though the question doesn't ask you specifically to include it, the examiner reading your work will be looking for such things. These are things that are needed to get a 9 for task fulfilment and, theoretically, anyone, whatever their level of English, should be able to get a good mark here.

4. The opening greeting of the letter

Your letter will probably need to be a reasonably informal letter to a friend or a semi-formal letter. The opening of your letter should reflect which one you are writing.

A friendly letter will open with Dear followed by a name which should then be followed by a comma, eg:

Dear John,

A semi-formal letter will also open with Dear and then be followed by a name, (if you decide that in the situation you would know the name) or by Sir (if it's a man), Madam (if it's a woman) or Sir/Madam if you don't know, eg:

Dear Mr. Phillips,

Dear Mrs. Phillips,

Dear Sir,

Dear Madam,

Dear Sir/Madam,

The question also might specify how you are to begin so follow what it says.

5. The opening paragraph of the letter

In a semi-formal letter, I feel it is important to state the reason for the letter straight away. You could use the following to help you:

I am writing to ask/ tell//inform you that...

I am writing to ask/inquire...

I am writing with regard to...

I am writing with reference to...

I am writing in connection with...

I am writing in response to...

In reply to your letter, I am writing to... (if the question indicates that you have had a letter)

If the letter is a less formal one to a friend then you should open the letter in a friendlier way e.g.:

Dear Anil,

Hi there! It's been so long since I've heard from you. I hope you are doing well and I hope all you family are doing fine. I'm pretty good in spite of working hard. Anyway, the reason I'm writing is...

6. The substance of the letter

I've already gone into the details about answering the question fully and using your imagination to produce a realistic letter fulfilling all functions so I won't repeat that. Through a great experience with the IELTS, I can say that questions tend to ask you to do certain things. Here I will give you some ideas about some language to use in the substance of the letter which will help you to answer the task well.

Asking for help

I would like you to...

I would be grateful if you could...

I need to ask your advice about...

I'd like to ask for information about...

What I'm looking for is...

Complaining

I'm writing to express my dissatisfaction/annoyance/ about...

I'm writing to express my anger at...

I am not happy about...

... is not what I expected/was expecting.

I want to know what you are going to do about this situation.

Thanking

I'm very grateful for...

I'd like to thank you very much for...

I very much appreciated...

Apologizing

I'm very sorry that/about...

Please forgive me for...

I'd like to apologize about...

Please accept my apologies

5. Ending your letter

First of all, in English we often end letters before the sign off with certain phrases. These can be included in most letters and will make your letter seem realistic and polished. For a formal letter, you could use:

If you require any further information, please do not hesitate to contact me. Thanking you in advance for your help, I look forward to hearing from you soon.

For a more informal letter you could use:

If you need to know anything else, just get in touch with me as soon as you can. Thanks a lot for your help and I hope to hear from you soon.

Be careful though! IELTS examiners quite rightly look for writing that has been memorised and just repeated so, if you use expressions like the ones above, make sure that they fit in with the rest of your letter.

Finally, you'll need to sign off your letter. For a formal letter, use:

Yours faithfully, OR

Yours sincerely,

Remember, the commas (it makes a good impression on the examiner if you use good punctuation) and spell "sincerely" correctly (a lot of people don't!).

For an informal letter, love is not always appropriate though English speakers use it a lot. Better would be to use:

Regards,

Yours,

Best wishes,

Other Hints for the IELTS General Training Task 1 Writing

1. DON'T copy any part of the question in your answer. This is not your own work and therefore, will be disregarded by the examiner and deducted from the word count. You can use individual words, but be careful of using "chunks" of the question text.

2. Don't repeat yourself or the same ideas. This gives a bad impression and the examiner realises that it isn't adding to the content of your letter.

3. If you are weak at English grammar, try to use short sentences. This allows you to control the grammar and the meaning of your writing much more easily and contributes to a better coherence and cohesion mark. It's much easier to make things clear in a foreign language, if you keep your sentences short!

4. Think about the tenses of your verbs. If you're writing about something that happened in the past, your verbs will need to be in the past tenses. If you're arranging something in the future, you will need to use the future tenses. If it's a habitual action, you'll need the present simple tense and so on. If you have time, a quick check of your verbs at the end of the exams can help you find errors.

5. Don't be irrelevant. Although you can use your imagination to expand on your answer, if any part of your letter is totally unrelated to the question, and put into just put up the word count, then the examiner will not take it into account and deduct it from the word count.

ABSTRACT

IELTS GENERAL WRITING includes two tasks. Task 1 is a GENERAL LETTER WRITING/Task 2 is a ESSAY WRITING. In this chapter, we are providing strategies (tricks to solve task 1) along with solved and practice tasks related to letter writing which clearly convince the students that how to crack the Task 1 in General Module.

SOLVED LETTER WRITING FOR WRITING TASK–1

LETTER–1

Your neighbours have recently written you a complaint about the noise from your flat. Write a letter to your neighbours. In your letter, explain the reasons for the noise and apologise. Describe what actions you will take in future to reduce the noise.

Write at least 150 words.

Dear Sachin,

I was shocked to get your letter saying that the noise from my flat has been spoiling your evenings and causing you some distress. I am really, really sorry about that and I hope you will accept my apologies.

As you may have guessed, I am trying to refit my kitchen in the evenings when I get home from work. Unfortunately it is all getting longer than expected and I have been facing problems with getting things to fit properly. This has meant to a lot of banging and hammering.

As the kitchen is still not finished, I have decided to call in a professional builder carpenter who will finish the work in the next day or two. He'll work only during daytime hours, so you won't be disturbed in the evenings again, I promise.

Sorry to have caused these problems,

Apoorv

LETTER–2

You will move to a new city for work. You know some people who live there. Ask them for help finding accommodation. Tell them, where you would like to live. Tell them the type of place you are looking for, etc.

Write at least 150 words.

Dear Sir,

I wanted to let you know that I am coming to live in (name of the city) and I would like to ask if you can help me with a few things before I arrive and start my new job.

Do you think you could give me a hand finding somewhere to live? Ideally, I would like to live close to where I am going to be working, or in the downtown street. If possible, I would like to be near some shops, like a supermarket or a DVD rental place. As I really love sports, it would be great to be near a park too.

I'm not too worried about the place itself. Obviously, I will be looking for a flat, rather than a house, as it is just going to be me and I won't be able to afford too much. So, a place with one bedroom is fine, but I would like to have a private bathroom (not shared), a kitchen and some kind of living room. It doesn't matter if the kitchen is small, but it would nice to have one. I would prefer to live somewhere new, so anything in a modern apartment block would be great.

Thanks for your help,

Robin

LETTER–3

Your car is hired from a company and while you are driving on a holiday, you meet with a small accident. You will have to write a report to the company to explain it. You need to explain the following:

When and where you hired it?

Describe how the accident happened.

What kind of actions did you take after the accident?

Dear Sir,

I am a recent customer of your rental company and I rented a car from your downtown outlet in South Delhi. The car hired was an economy model vehicle which I rented from March 21st to the present. I would like to commend your company on their professionalism and the service offered, and as such, I am sure you will handle my incident with these qualities.

Unfortunately, I had an unavoidable accident involving the aforementioned vehicle and another party. The accident was caused by the other car failing to stop at the red light of the intersection, I was passing through, and as such, the second party collided into the driver's side of my automobile. The police were informed about the mishappening, whereupon they recorded information regarding the accident and the other driver's insurance details.

The police established the other driver's responsibility for the accident, and the second party's insurance company has been informed. I would like to request that a replacement vehicle be offered while my current vehicle is incapacitated. I shall be really thankful to you.

Yours sincerely,

Akshay Ahuja

LETTER–4

You should spend about 20 minutes on this task.

You had a good meal in a local restaurant with your family. Write a letter to the newspaper to tell them about it, describe the meal you had, and why you think the restaurant is worth visiting.

You should write at least 150 words.

To the Editor,

I am a long standing member of our local community and I am writing a recommendation to other citizens for one of our fine neighbourhood dining establishments; *The Cyber Cafe*.

There were many impressive attributes which struck me upon my entrance, such as the décor and the ambience. I particularly enjoyed the laid back attitude of the place. But for my mind, it was the service along with the size and quality of the portions that was the most memorable.

The service was professional yet intimate, and along with the sheer quantity of the dishes served, motivated me to pass on my recommendation. I enjoyed a steak of mammoth proportions and a giant fresh, crisp salad accompanied by a selection of appropriately selected seasonal vegetables. The piece of resistance, however, was the rich Black Forest served as dessert –and all this for a reasonable price.

I hope after reading this, potential customers will frequent to have dinner here.

Yours truly,

Tini Alia

LETTER–5

You should spend about 20 minutes on this task.

Write a letter to complain about a situation in which some adolescents let their dogs run wildly causing dangerous situations and describe what is the situation, how the situation got under control what are the necessary steps taken.

You should write at least 150 words.

Dear Sir/Madam,

I am writing to draw your attention to a situation that has been developing in my neighbourhood. Recently, I have witnessed many dogs on the loose in the neighbourhood.

The dogs, which are fierce looking and not muzzled, are given licensce and freedom to run around the neighbourhood. They are intimidating, especially to children and the elderly. I am afraid that it's just a matter of time before someone gets seriously injured.

The owners of these dogs, a bunch of adolescents, seem to be unaware of the dangers of letting their pets off the leash and have adopted a non-chalant attitude. The teenagers have been asked by numerous locals to keep the dogs under control, but all requests have been ignored and the situation has not improved. I, therefore, believe that immediate action must be taken and request you to investigate the matter and take appropriate actions as soon as possible to prevent the occurrence of injury and serious bodily harm to the people in and around the locality.

Yours sincerely,

Manik Chaudhary

LETTER–6

You ordered a new cheque book from your bank, two weeks ago, but you have received nothing. Write a letter to the manager complaining about the bad service. Say when and how you ordered the cheque book. Ask how much longer you will have to wait and ask the manager what actions he will take over this matter.

Dear Sir,

I am writing to complain about the service that I have received at your bank. Two weeks ago, I ordered a cheque book by filling out the appropriate form when I visited the bank, but since then, I have not received the cheque book and I have received no other correspondence from the bank. It is quite urgent for me as I have quite a few bills that I need to pay that can only be paid by cheque.

Please write to me as soon as possible and let me know how much longer I will have to wait for my cheque book and please explain why I have had to wait so long. I would also like to know what actions, you are going to take regarding this bad service.

I have been a customer of your bank now for 15 years, and this is the first time I have had to complain. It is very disappointing.

I look forward to hearing from you soon.

Yours sincerely,

Anil Sakeri

LETTER–7

You would like to buy some electrical goods at a shop in a nearby town. Write a letter to the shop and ask if they have the things you want, or whether they will be able to order them. Ask what the prices are, and how long they will be able to hold the goods for you.

Dear Sir,

I am writing to enquire if you have various electrical goods that I want to buy. I have tried shops in my own town, but they don't have exactly what I want.

I want the new Sony DVD player, (A Tablet) and a radio with long wave capability. Do you have these items in stock or, if not, will you be able to order them soon? I also need to know what price you charge for these items? If you do have these things, would you be able to hold them for me and for how long? I am free this weekend and, if you have them, I can come over on Saturday morning to pay you and pick them up.

Please write back to me as soon as possible at the above address or call me on my mobile number (07364 957 143). I look forward to hearing from you soon.

Yours sincerely,

Sunidhi Singh

LETTER–8

You have been invited to attend an interview for a place studying a course in a college. Unfortunately, because of a previous appointment, you cannot come at the time they wish. Write a letter to the admissions tutor and explain your position. Apologise and offer to come on another day or later the same day. Ask also, how long the interview will be and whether there will be any tests during it.

Dear Sir,

Thank you very much for your letter dated 15th May inviting me for an interview at your college on Wednesday 2nd June at 10am. I am extremely sorry but I am unable to come to an interview at that time because I have a Maths exam that morning. I cannot miss this exam, but of course, I really wish to attend the interview with you. Is it possible that I could come to the interview the same day but in the afternoon? Failing that, I would be able to come the next day or any day after.

I would also like to ask some things about the interview. I would like to know how long it will last and also whether, I will be required to clear any tests during it.

Once again I apologise for not being able to attend the interview at the time that you wanted and I hope, I will be able to meet with you at another time. I look forward to hearing from you soon.

Yours sincerely,
Saini Kakker

LETTER–9

A friend of yours is going on holiday soon and has asked you to recommend a destination. Write a letter to your friend and recommend a good place for a holiday that you have visited before. Say where you went, where you stayed, what you did there and how was the food like.

Write at least 150 words.

Dear Anuj,

Thanks for your letter. I'm glad and hope you and your family are well. So, you're thinking of going on holiday in the UK. Well I can certainly recommend one destination for you. I went one year to a place called Lochinver in the north-west of Scotland. It's quite a long trip to get there, as it's only about 30 miles from the north coast, but it's worth it.

There are only a few places to stay. There are two hotels, the Kirkaig and the Assynt in the centre of the town, and a campsite just outside town. We stayed at the Kirkaig Hotel but I know you and your family are keen campers, so you might prefer the camping option.

There is a lot to do but it's a bit dependent on the weather. There's a beautiful beach, a golf course, the fishing is excellent and there are fantastic hills nearby for walking amidst amazing scenery. If it's wet, there's a small cinema in town but that's about all. Take some board games!

The food is typical British in the hotels, but some of the Scottish specialities are fantastic. If you're camping though, food will be up to you!

Anyway, I've got to go out now and pick up the kids. Write again if you need any more information.

Regards,

Simar

LETTER–10

You have just spent a weekend staying at the Premier Inn in Dubai. When you get home you find that you have left a bag at the hotel. Describe in detail, where you left the bag and describe the bag with your personal request.

Write at least 150 words on how you would recover your bag.

Spend around 20 minutes on this task.

Dear Mr. Singh,

I stayed in your hotel on the 23rd and 24th of October. I was in Room No. 603. When I arrived home, I discovered that I had left one of my bag at the hotel. Could you please check from your 'Lost and Found Department' and see if my bag is there?

The bag is a small black leather, document case with a narrow strap. Inside the bag, you will find several business cards, a fountain pen, a small address book, three copies of a business proposal and a silver pocket calculator. These things are not very valuable in terms of money, but they have a lot of personal value.

I would appreciate it if you could contact me as soon as possible, particularly, since I need the proposals for a presentation this week. If you could send the bag to me by courier service, I would be most grateful. I have arranged to pay for the service.

Thank you for your help.

Yours sincerely,
Rohan Sapra

LETTER–11

One of your friends wants to apply for a job involving working with foreign teenagers. Write a letter of recommendation for him/her.

Write at least 150 words.

You should spend about 20 minutes on this task.

Dear Sir or Madam,

I have learnt from your newspaper advertisement that your center is organizing an international summer camp for overseas teenagers, and you are looking for a bilingual assistant tutor to work with the children. I am writing to you to recommend one of my best friends, *Vanshika Chaturvedi*, for this post.

Vanshika Chaturvedi used to be my classmate at the Delhi University, where she was already a very active organizer and participant in extracurricular activities. With her outstanding leadership skills and cheerful personality, she was elected chairperson of the Student Union several times.

Busy as she was, she passed the College English Test Band Six and completed her major – teenage psychology – with an excellent school record. Upon graduation, she was assigned to be a teacher in an international high school in South Delhi, where she has been teaching bilingual lessons for five years. What's more, she loves her job and enjoys working with children. This has won her great popularity among her students.

Therefore, I do not hesitate to recommend her as an ideal candidate for the post you advertised. I am sure you will make a wise decision in hiring her.

Yours sincerely,

Nidhi Singh

LETTER–12

You want to apply for the following job. Write a letter to Mr. Moore describing your previous experience and explaining why you would be suitable for the job. Waiter/Waitress required for evening work. Some experience necessary.

Write at least 150 words.

Spend around 20 minutes on this task.

Dear Mr. Moore,

Re: (Waitress position) I am writing to express my interest in your recently advertised position for a waitress. Enclosed with this letter is my resume, which further furnish details of my previous experience and qualifications.

Not only that, as for as my qualifications and work experience are concerned, it makes me a perfect candidate for the job. My personality is well suited to working as a waitress. I am a very friendly person who can quickly establish rapport with people of all ages. In my last waitress job, I had over a dozen repeat customers each day. And, the fast-paced environment of waiting on tables suits me well, because I thrive on working under pressure. In fact, my former boss was surprised at both my incredible stamina and efficiency in dealing with customers' orders.

I would like to meet with you at your earliest convenience, to discuss the possibility of working at your restaurant.

Thank you for your consideration of my application. I look forward to meeting you in the near future.

Yours sincerely,

Saini Takker

PRACTICE SESSION
FOR WRITING TASK–1

1. *You have a friend who is about to enter the university, and he wants you to advise him on which subject to specialize in – history, in which he is very interested, or computer science, which offers better job prospects.*
2. *After being involved in an accident, you were looked after by another person. Write a special letter to express your thanks.*
3. *One of your pen pals will shortly be visiting your city. For some reasons, you can not manage to meet him at the airport on time.*
4. *Your find that your study load is too heavy. Write a letter to your college teacher explaining why you need to withdraw from two courses. Ask if it is possible to obtain a refund.*
5. *As part of a student social survey project, you are organizing a group to visit a historical exhibition in a small town. Write a letter asking for information regarding such things, as the contents of the exhibition, and the dates of its opening and closing, and also, if there are any discounts available.*
6. *You live in a room of a college, where you share it with another student. You find it very difficult to work there because your roommate always has friends visiting. He/She has parties in the room and sometimes, borrows your things without asking you.*
7. *Write a letter to the Accommodation Officer at the college and ask for a new room next term. You would prefer a single room. Explain your reasons.*

ABSTRACT

Here, the candidate will get solved examples of Task-2 for writing which has been shortlisted from the previous exams. These solved writing tasks will help in building the skills of writing among the IELTS candidates.

SOLVED ESSAY
WRITING TASK –2

TOPIC NO. 1
GROWTH OF COMPUTERS

You should spend about 40 minutes on this task.Write about the following topic:

School children are becoming far too dependent on computers. This is having an alarming effect on reading and writing skills. Teachers need to avoid using computers in the classroom at all costs and go back to the teaching basic study skills.Do you agree or disagree?

Give reasons for your answer and include any relevant examples from your own knowledge or experience. Write at least 250 words.

Nowadays, modern technology has totally changed our approach to wards study. In many countries, students no longer have to copy notes by hand from the blackboard; instead the teacher gives them a photocopy. Rather than messy ink and pen, students present a typed-up copy of their assignments. Their computer even checks their spellings as they go. In fact, some people believe that modern technology does a lot of our thinking for us and, as a result, we are going to loose our ability to think for ourselves.

In my opinion, spelling skills have definitely deteriorated in the recent years. So many the young people use mobile phones to send text messages where speed and conciseness are more important than spelling or grammar. Some teachers complain that these students take the same attitude towards their assignments.

On the other hand, typed assignments are much easier to read. Frankly, I find some notes or texts which are handwritten almost impossible to read. Doctors, for example, have a reputation for illegible handwriting, which could lead to disastrous medical mistakes. Perhaps, it is time we focussed not on handwriting, but on presenting information as accurately as possible.

One advantage of computers is that access to the Internet has opened up a new world of learning for us. We no longer have to wait for a book that has already been borrowed from the library before we do our research. In fact, the Internet can clearly be used to research information in the same way as a library, but more conveniently. On the whole, rather than holding students back, I believe that the modern technology has actually improved standards of education considerably.

TOPIC NO. 2

UNSUSTAINABLE POPULATION GROWTH

You should spend about 40 minutes on this task.Write about the following topic:

Countries, such as China, India and Japan have unsustainable population growths. In fact, many experts are of the opinion that the population 'explosion' which is now a very worrying concern, is the most serious threat to life on this planet. Give some suggestions to address this problem.

Write at least 250 words.

It is true that the population 'explosion' which has taken place over the last century, is a very serious problem. One of the main reasons for this unacceptable population growth is a lack of understanding about the environment. Overpopulation is the major reason for water, soil and air pollution. It is also often the cause of starvation and even wars. Experts have put forward many suggestions to address this problem. The following are just a few of these.

The most important weapon we have to fight population growth is *education*. This should start at a very early age, i.e., before children even go to school. TV cartoons and children's programs can be used to educate the very young. At, high school level, students can be taught about the problem more directly. At, university level, scholarships should be made available to students who wish to study further in this field. International exchange groups may also help to increase awareness.

Another important means of controlling population growth is to disadvantage people who have more than one or two children. This can be done, as it is in China, by means of a higher tax. Although it is controversial, persons who come forward to be sterilized could be given a sum of money. It may also be possible to make it advantageous for people to have only one child by giving such couples a special tax deduction.

It should also be possible to make contraception devices free to the public and easily obtainable.

This problem is a very difficult one to address but we should make every effort to do so. There are many other problems which are related to overpopulation, such as increasing crime, illiteracy and pollution. So by addressing one problem, we would be addressing the others as well.

TOPIC NO. 3
WORKING PARENTS

You should spend about 40 minutes on this task.Write about the following topic:

In today's competitive world, many families find it necessary for both parents to go out to work. While some say the children in these families benefit from the additional income, others feel they lack support because of their parents' absence.

Give reasons for your answer and include any relevant examples from your own knowledge or experience.Write at least 250 words.

In the past, a typical family consisted of a father who went out to work and a mother who stayed at home and looked after the children. Nowadays, in the big towns, cities and metrocities, it is the norm for both parents to work. This situation can affect children, both positively and negatively.

Some people think that the children of working parents are in an advantageous position, where their parents are able to afford mere luxuries, such as new clothes, video games or mobile phones. Proponents of this view argue that children are able to enjoy and experience more from life due to their parents' extra wealth, for example, by going on foreign holidays.

On the other hand, however, there are those who claim that when both parents work, their children do not get enough support and attention, meaning that the children might not do as well at school because there is no one at house to provide support with such things as homework or exam revision. The absence of a parent at home could make it easier for children to get involved in such things as drugs or undertake drinking.

When I was growing up, both my parents worked and I was always well provided for. On the other hand, I think that it would sometimes have been better if I could have seen more of my parents' precious.

In conclusion, I believe that we cannot change the fact that both parents have to work nowadays. It is not an ideal situation, but if parents spare time for their children in the evenings and at the weekends, then the children will not suffer in any way. It must be stated that the extra income generated by both the parents working, makes for a much higher standard of living which definitely benefits the whole family.

TOPIC NO. 4

BOOKS *vs* EXPERIENCE

You should spend about 40 minutes on this task. Write about the following topic:

It has been said, "Not every thing that is learnt is contained in books" Compare and contrast the knowledge gained from experience with knowledge gained from books. In your opinion, which source is more important? Why?

Give reasons for your answer and include any relevant examples from your own knowledge or experience. Write at least 250 words.

"Experience is the best teacher" ways an old cliché, and I totally agree with it. The most important, and sometimes the hardest, lessons we learn in life come from our participation in situations. You can' learn everything from a book.

Of course, learning from books in a formal educational setting is also valuable. It's in schools that we learn the information we need to function in our society. We learn how to speak and write and understand mathematical equations. These are all the information we need to live in our communities and earn a living.

Nevertheless, I think that the most important lessons can't be taught; they have to be experienced. No one can teach us how to get along with others or how to have self-respect. As we grow from children into teenagers, no one can teach us how to deal with peer pressure. As we leave adolescence behind and enter the adult life, no one can teach us how to fall in love and get married.

This shouldn't stop us from looking for guidelines along the way. Teachers and parents are valuable sources of advice when we're young. As we enter into the new stages in our lives, the advice we receive from them is very helpful because they have already had similar experiences. But experiencing our own triumphs and disasters is really the only way to learn how to deal with life.

TOPIC NO. 5

FOOD *vs* STANDARD OF LIVING

You should spend about 40 minutes on this task. Write about the following topic:

Nowadays, food has become easier to prepare. Has this change improved the way people live? Use specific reasons and examples to support your answer.

Give reasons for your answer and include any relevant examples from your own knowledge or experience. Write at least 250 words.

The 20th century has brought with it many advances. With those advances, human lives have changed dramatically. In some ways life is worse, but mostly, it is better. Changes in food preparation methods have improved our lives greatly.

The convenience of preparing food today is amazing. Even stoves have gotten too slow for us. Microwave cooking is much easier. We can press a few buttons and a meal is completely cooked in just a short time. People used to spend hours preparing an oven-cooked meal, and now they can use that time for other, better things. Plus, there are all kinds of portable, prepackaged foods we can buy. Heat them in the office microwave, and lunch at work is quick and easy.

Food preparation today allows for more variety. With refrigerators and freezers, we can preserve a lot of different foods in our homes. Since technology makes cooking so much faster, people are willing to make several dishes for even a small meal. Parents are more likely to let children be picky, now that they can easily heat them up some prepackaged macaroni and cheese on the side. Needless to say, adults living in the same house may have very different eating habits as well. If they don't want to cook a lot of different dishes, it's common now to eat out at restaurants several times a week.

Healthful eating is also easier than ever now. When people cook, they use new fat substitutes and cooking sprays to cut fat and calories. This reduces the risk of heart disease and high cholesterol. Additionally, we can buy fruits and vegetables fresh, frozen or canned. They are also easy to prepare, and so many of us eat more of those nutritious items daily. A hundred years ago, you couldn't imagine the process of taking some frozen fruits and ice creams from the freezer, adding some low-fat yogurt from a plastic cup and some juice from a can in the refrigerator, and whipping up a low-fat in the blender!

Our lifestyle is fast, but people still like good food. What new food preparation technology has given us is more choices. *Today, we can prepare food that is more convenient, healthier, and of greater variety than ever before in history.*

TOPIC NO. 6

HAZARDS OF HEALTH

You should spend about 40 minutes on this task.Write about the following topic:

In many countries of today, due to sedentary life the eating habits and lifestyle of children are different from those of previous generations. Some people say this has had a negative effect on their health.To what extent do you agree or disagree with this opinion?

Give reasons for your answer and include any relevant examples from your own knowledge or experience. Write at least 250 words.

There is plenty of evidence to suggest that children are overweight and the situation is getting worse, according to the medical experts. I feel there are a number of reasons for this.

Some people blame the fact that we are surrounded by shops selling unhealthy, fatty foods, such as chips and fried chicken, at low prices. This has created a whole generation of adults who have never cooked a meal for themselves. If there were fewer of these restaurants, then children would not be tempted to buy take-away food.

There is another argument that blames the parents for allowing their children to become overweight. I tend to agree with this view, because good eating habits begin early in life, long before children start to visit fast food outlets. If children are given chips and chocolate rather than nourishing food, or are always allowed to choose what they eat, they will go for the sweet and salty foods every time, and this will carry on throughout their lives.

There is a third factor, however, which contributes to the situation. Children these days take very little exercise. They do not walk to school. When they reach home, they sit in front of the television, or in front of their computers and play video games. There activities will inturn couch potatoes. Not only is this an unhealthy pastime, it also gives them time to eat more junk food. What they need is to go outside and play active games or sports.

The two views discussed play an equal role in contributing to the problem, but I think, we have to encourage young people to be more active, as well as help steering them away from fast food outlets and bad eating habits. We need to have a balanced approach.

TOPIC NO. 7
IMPORTANCE OF HOLIDAYS

You should spend about 40 minutes on this task.

According to those in the travel business, the nature of the average 'holiday' is changing. Rather than seeking a relaxing break in a faraway place, people now want excitement on their holidays and are keen to participate in unusual and challenging activities. Do you agree or disagree?

You should write at least 250 words.

Holidays are important because they provide a break from our normal daily routine and from the world of work. Traditionally, holidays have been seen as a time for relaxation and as an opportunity to visit another country in order to find out about its geography and customs. Nowadays, however, it seems that other types of holidays are becoming popular.

Some people want their holiday to be a kind of adventure, and find this more exciting than going to the beach or visiting museums. On an adventure holiday, you may stay in a quiet basic accommodation, rather than a luxurious hotel. Activities may involve things, such as bush walking or cycling, or may form part of an aid project designed to help communities in remote areas. Holidays, such as these are popular with people of all ages and can often, help to promote tourism in rural environments.

The increasing popularity of dangerous sports has also boosted the number of adventure holidays; for example, water sports, mountain climbing or paragliding. These holidays are more popular with the younger generation, as they can be both physically and mentally demanding. Participants are often seeking the sort of thrills that they cannot get in ordinary life.

There is now greater awareness of the damaging effects of mass tourism and this may be one reason for the changing nature of holidays. This can only be a good thing. But perhaps, people are also discovering that it is just as refreshing to take an active holiday, as it is to lie on a beach - though that is still a question of personal preference.

TOPIC NO. 8

ORIGINAL IDEAS *vs* COPIED IDEAS

You should spend about 40 minutes on this task.

In certain cases, it has been seen, original ideas with new concepts flourishes more as compared to the copied ones. For example, the concept of using smart mobile phones have really changed the lives of the people. So without any doubt, I must say original ideas are far better than the copied ones, as it more existable than the copied ones.

You should write at least 250 words.

I certainly agree that people who come up with new and original ideas; in other words, those who 'invent' or 'discover' things are terribly important to society as a whole. However, I also think there is a role in the society for good imitators.

No one would deny that the key individuals must be thanked for providing us with certain facilities that we use everyday. Where, would we be, for example, without basic items, such as the washing machine, the television and, more recently, the computer? These items are now used so regularly that we tend to take them for granted.

In fact, thc socicty wc livc in today has bccomc increasingly consumer-oriented, and while it may be possible to constantly update and improve consumer goods, not everyone where I live can afford the prices of these innovations. Furthermore, not everyone lives in an area that has accessibility to the latest models on the market. For this reason, there is a value to be placed on being able to provide good copies of expensive items.

Having said that, certain innovations have a more serious impact on our lives than consumer goods and cannot easily be replicated. Vital medicines like penicillin and vaccines against dangerous diseases also exist because people made continual efforts to develop them. Scientific ideas, such as these enable us to live longer and escape illnesses.

TOPIC NO. 9

MEANS OF TRANSPORT

You should spend about 40 minutes on this task.

Discuss the advantages and disadvantages of having a car.

You should write at least 250 words.

Give reasons for your answer and include relevant examples.

Car is a major necessity and the most important means of transport in today's world. Driving in a four-wheeler not only provides you the status of a luxurious life, but also provides comfort in all seasons of life whether in the time of emergency, or moving to and fro at far off places, etc.

The main advantage of the car is that it gives the freedom to travel when and where you want, without being limited to fixed routes and timetables. What is more, you can carry several passengers and as much luggage as you like, at no extra cost. In addition to this, you can travel in comfort in a car, with a seat to yourself and the possibility of comforts, such as a music system and air conditioning.

On the other hand, owning a car is very expensive. Moreover, the price of the car, the cost of tax, insurance, petrol and repairs must also be considered before buying. Moreover, the increase in traffic means that drivers are spending more and more time stuck in traffic jams. Perhaps, the major disadvantage of cars in general is the huge damage that they do to human life and to the environment, and all motorists must accept that they are making a small contribution to this.

To sum up, have access to an efficient public transport system, then buying and running your own car could be considered an expensive luxury.

TOPIC NO. 10

NATURE *vs* NURTURE

You should spend about 40 minutes on this task.

Research indicates that the characteristics we have been with have much more influence on our personality and development than any experience, we may have in our lives; which do you consider to be the major influence?

You should write at least 250 words.

Today, the way we consider human psychology and mental development is heavily influenced by the genetic sciences. We now understand the importance of inherited characteristics more than ever before. Yet we are still unable to decide whether an individual's personality and development are more influenced by genetic factors (nature) or by the environment (nurture).

Research, relating to identical twins, has highlighted how significant inherited characteristics can be for an individual's life. But whether these characteristics are able to develop within the personality of an individual surely depends on whether the circumstances allow such a development. It seems that the experiences we have in life are so unpredictable and powerful, that they can boost or override other influences, and there seems to be plenty of research findings to confirm this.

My own view is that there is no one major influence in a person's life. Instead, the traits we inherit from our parents and the situations and experiences that we encounter in life are constantly interacting. It is the interaction of the two that shapes a person's personality and dictates how that personality develops. If this were not true, we would be able to predict the behaviour and character of a person from the moment they were born.

Personality is something skin deep. It builds according to the charisma and persona of a person. It basically depends upon in what type of environment we are nurturing. Some personality traits we get from nature, i.e., Physical development of the body, intelligence, sharpness, etc. and some from we get from nurturing in a particular family, for e.g. if father is a doctor, automatically he/she nurtures their child to develop in the field of medicine itself.

In conclusion, I do not think that either nature or nurture is the major influence on a person, but that both have powerful effects. How these factors interact is still unknown today and they remain largely unpredictable in a person's life.

TOPIC NO. 11

PUNISHMENT TO MURDERERS

You should spend about 40 minutes on this task.

By punishing murderers with the death penalty, the society is also guilty of committing murder. Therefore, life in prison is a better punishment for murderers. To what extent do you agree or disagree with this statement?

You should write at least 250 words. Give reasons for your answer and include any relevant examples from your own knowledge or experience.

I strongly support the death penalty for murderers. In today's society, life is very violent. There are many mentally-ill people committing crimes and almost nothing will stop them. We have interviewed captured criminals who say, "I was going to kill him, but I knew that I could get the death penalty if I did. So I just left him there." Obviously, having the death penalty saves lives and that makes a positive difference to the society.

If a criminal does murder someone, and then gets the death penalty, that isn't the society's fault. Everyone knows about the death penalty as a punishment for murder. So, the person who murders is really killing himself at the same time he is killing his victim. The murderer has made the choice to die.

It is important to remember that the death penalty is used only for people who have committed very serious crimes. For example, a woman shot a police officer when she was trying to escape from jail. She was already a convicted criminal when she committed murder, and she deserves the death penalty. On the other side of the coin, life imprisonment, no doubt is a good punishment for murderers, but in those cases, who are ready to reform themselves not for those who are ready to commit these crimes again and again. A punishment of death penalty will save the society from the cruelty of humanity on this earth.

People need to accept the responsibilties for their respective actions. Punishing murderers with the death penalty is one way by which the society can help people to realise the consequences of their decisions.

TOPIC NO. 12

COMPETITION *vs* COOPERATION

You should spend about 40 minutes on this task.

Some people think that a sense of competition in children should be encouraged. Others believe that children who are taught to cooperate rather than compete become more useful adults. Discuss both these views and give your own opinion.

You should write at least 250 words. Give reasons for your answer and include any relevant examples from your own knowledge or experience.

Nowadays, the purpose of education is being changed in the Metropolis. There are some people who think that competition in children should be made, also others believe that children who are taught to cooperate become more useful adults. There are advantages and disadvantages for both of the arguments.

To begin with, what is good if a sense of competition in children is made? They could develop themselves more and more as they learn and study a lot to win from the competition. To prove this, in metropolis it is popular - even common now - to have a tutor who comes to the student's house to teach the extra pieces of study and makes a lot of money. They learn faster than what they learn at school. Furthermore, during the vacations, students study abroad to learn English for a month instead of revise school work. If they have experiments such as study abroad, it is one of the greatest plus point to go to the famous well-known high-school. Moreover, there are four big school exams and two national examinations to test students' level of studies. Generally, only the highest 40% can go to the good quality of highschools and colleges. Children learn as much as they can, to win the competition to obtain good quality schools.

On the other hand, as they are busy to enter the schools and study individually with their own tutors, there are problems. They become selfish. They become careless and don't help others alot if it is about studies. There will be no cooperations among them. But cooperation is necessary than competing. People talk and listen to others thoughts and learn. These can also be a great opportunity to learn instead of learning alone with one teacher.

In conclusion, I strongly agree that children should be taught to cooperate, rather than compete. *Nobody is perfect. People learn together, work together to develop each other.* Therefore, I want parents and teachers to educate children concentrating on cooperation, not competing and ranking them. An if at all, these should be a competitions; it should be a healthy competition.

TOPIC NO. 13

TRAFFIC & HOUSING PROBLEMS

You should spend about 40 minutes on this task.

Traffic and housing problems in major cities could be solved by moving large companies and factories and their employees to the countryside.To what extent do you agree or disagree with this opinion?

You should write at least 250 words. Give reasons for your answer and include any relevant examples from your own knowledge or experience.

These days with the increasing urban populations, there are major problems with congestion and not only the price, but also availability of accommodation in large cities of the world. It seems that one possible solution could be to relocate large companies and factories as well as their respective employees out of these urban areas into more rural ones. In my opinion, I strongly agree that this would have a desired effect in making cities more livable.

To begin with, the traffic problem in cities doesn't only exist from commuting employees, but also the general public travelling around the city. While this may be a fact, if the number of workers' vehicles are reduced on city streets, a large percentage of traffic will obviously decline in rush hours. For example, the peak hour traffic is undoubtedly made up largely of the staff from companies going to and from home. So, in order to overcome the traffic congestion during peak hours, Metro Trains have today become the only solution for daily commuters.

Secondly, with regard to housing problems, the population will always continue to grow in cities and therefore, inadvertently decrease the number of cheap and available apartments. This is certainly obvious, however, as a large proportion of these apartments are occupied by employees from large firms and their families. If this workforce is relocated to housing estates in the country, city apartment blocks will fall in price and certainly increase in availability.

In conclusion, by relocating workers to rural areas to work and reside, heavy traffic conditions and lack of adequate accommodation in city centres will obviously change for the better. As far as I'm concerned, I agree that the government should enforce such a law in order to increase our standards of living in our hectic city life of today.

TOPIC NO. 14

SENIORITY *vs* MERIT

You should spend about 40 minutes on this task.

Companies should encourage employees who work in a high position to leave or retire at the age of 55 in order to give opportunities to the new generation. To what extent do you agree or disagree with this opinion?

You should write at least 250 words.

Give reasons for your answer and include any relevant examples from your own knowledge or experience.

I totally disagree with the idea of high-level employees leaving at the age of 55 to make room for the upcoming generation. While it is true that the energy level and fresh ideas of youth can rejuvenate a company, the steady hand of experience can still best guide a company in most cases.

In English there is a saying, "You can't teach an old dog new tricks." In the fast-paced world of business, bolstered by even faster hi-tech innovations, a younger more pliant mind would seem to be able to adapt with greater flexibility, but very rigid for the older one to adopt it. Take, for example, the Microsoft's Bill Gates, whose energy and brilliant insights as a youth helped him to pioneer new territories in the computer software world and establish a digital empire. Now as a more mature CEO, this kind of the "computer" mountain is constantly on the verge of being knocked down by the upcoming digital entrepreneurs. However, it is now the experience he has accumulated as an older man which keeps him on the top. So, combining the vigour and innovation of younger workers with the experience of the older workers would seem to be the winning hand in the world of business.

The assertion is to give opportunities to the younger generation. If everyone retires at 55, there will be a smaller pool of experience at the company. So, who will show them the ropes of the trade? It would be as if we lopped off the last few chapters of a textbook. On this point, the argument would seem to be built on false presumptions.

And think of all the other problems, retirement at 55 would create. With life expectancy in many advanced nations at 70-plus years, how would the state along with private enterprises be able to support their retirement pensions? The economic repercussions of such an idea could be great.

Merit and competition are the two pillars of the western society, not the seniority. So if we do not agree that companies should not retire the employees at the age of 55, then somewhere we are taking huge turns from the pillars of the western society.

Granted, my counter-arguments are perhaps as simplistic as the original assertion itself, but without qualifying the assertion with greater supporting evidence or background information, both sides can be argued. Nevertheless, even after thoroughly considering the argument, I believe I would still adhere to my viewpoint that the assertion lacks merit for the aforementioned reasons. Besides, when I am 55, I do not fancy the idea of being put out to pasture. I think I will still be full of vitality and have a desire to work, so I hope my workplace will view me as a treasure house of valuable experience to pass along to the next generation and keep me on until I am at least 65, if not older.

TOPIC NO. 15
LANGUAGE TUSSLE

You should spend around 40 minutes on this task.

Some people think that it is important to have a single language as an international official language. Others think that it will make it difficult to identify countries and cause a loss of culture. What are your opinions on this?

You should write at least 250 words.

Give reasons for your answer and include any relevant examples from your own knowledge or experience.

With the advent of globalisation, a common language to facilitate trade and communication seems inevitable. Some oppose the development of a single language on the grounds that it may lead to cultural erosion and a loss of local linguistic knowledge. Yet, I am of the opinion that it is possible to use an official international language and still retain one's own language and culture.

Firstly, many countries already use an official language or languages. For example, in India there are *two official languages: Hindi and English*. In a country, such as India where there are innumerable languages spoken, there is a need for official languages to ensure communication between different sections of the population and the different states. In China, where different dialects are spoken, *Mandarin*, the official language, enables people from different provinces to comprehend each other.

Secondly, in an age of rampant globalisation, there is no doubt that an international language is inevitable. How is an African businessman going to conduct business in China when there are such differences between languages? In this sense, not only is an international language (mother tongue) inevitable, but also a necessity for trade, commerce and economic expansion in the 21st century. Moreover, it also increases tourism and foreign exchange of a particular country also but if there is a communication gap i.e. task of common language among the nations, then it would be really be hard for economic prosperity.

The critics opposing the adoption of an international official language argue that it would lead to a loss of cultural identity. However, the use of an international official language doesn't mean that mother languages will die out. For example, English already functions as a kind of unofficial international language, but this doesn't mean that people solely converse in English, or they neglect their own language. English is used in specific contexts (trade, business, etc) and native languages are used for everyday instructions.

In brief, as the world becomes smaller, the need for an official international language seems unavoidable. English has already assumed this role, although its status is unofficial. In my view, the use of either an official or unofficial international language is necessary to facilitate communication in a time of rapid globalisation.

TOPIC NO. 16

LARGE COMPANY *vs* SMALL COMPANY

You should spend about 40 minutes on this task.

Some people prefer to work for a large company. Others prefer to work for a small company. Which would you prefer? Use specific reasons and examples to support your choice.

You should write at least 250 words.

Give reasons for your answer and include any relevant examples from your own knowledge or experience.

The issue whether working for a large company is better than working for a small company is a controversial one. From my everyday experience and observations, I think that every option has its advantages and disadvantages. I base my opinion on the following points.

From the one side working for a large company brings many benefits and incentives. First of all, one has better medical insurance, higher salary with incentives, and often employees of a large company have less responsibilities. Moreover, they feel more secure because their company has more clients and this means better chance to survive on the modern market. However, one working for a large company has less chance to be promoted because onc's manager does not want to lose his or her job unless she or he is promoted too. Also, from my observations, managers of a large company do not pay much attention to one's solutions and suggestions.

From the other side, working for a small company has many advantages too. Firstly, one has better chance to be promoted. Secondly, one can talk to the owner of the company about any improvements that can be done in order to get more profits. Another important aspect of working for a small company is the opportunities to find out more about how company works. As a result of this, one can gain more experience and get better recommendations. However, this also has some disadvantages. For instance, one can get less salary, worse medical benefits, etc.

To sum up, I think that every person chooses for himself herself what he or she wants. If one wants better career and more responsibilities then a small company is a better choice. Otherwise, working for a large company may be a good option too.

TOPIC NO. 17

PERSONA OF CO-WORKERS

You should spend about 40 minutes on this task.

> *We all work or will work in our jobs with many different kinds of people. In your opinion, what are some important characteristics of a co-worker (someone you work closely with)? Use reasons and specific examples to explain why these characteristics are important.*

You should write at least 250 words.

A large number of people spend most of their time at work. Our life is divided into three equal parts: 8 hours - sleep, 8 hours - work, 8 hours - family time. So, in most of the cases, one's co-worker plays a significant role in one's life. From my opinion, the essential characteristics of a co-worker are the following.

First of all, a person who works closely with me must like his job. I think it is very important for a person to feel satisfied with his job. My husband is a software developer. He is fond of his job and people enjoy working with him because they see how much energy, he puts into his job.

Second by, my co-worker must be persistent and never give up. I like when people who came across a problem try to solve it, find a good decision instead of looking for another person to hand it over. Another important aspect of this is that a good worker should always ask himself, "What can be improved?" and suggests new solutions.

In addition, he must be a good team player. In the modern world, good communication skills and the ability to work in a team are among the common position requirements. Personally, I think it is great to help each other, share new ideas, develop new solutions, etc. It helps to create a team spirit and improve labour productivity.

Finally, my co-worker must be punctual. He or she should finish the job on time as I think that is unacceptable to make the rest of a team wait while a person finishes his or her job. Also, my "ideal co-worker" should always be ready to offer his or her help and be supportive.

To summarise, I think if a co-worker possesses all of these qualities mentioned above, he can make work with him really enjoyable and productive.

TOPIC NO. 18

CLASSMATES INFLUENCE MORE THAN PARENTS

You should spend about 40 minutes on this task.

Do you agree or disagree with the following statement? Classmates have more importance influence rather than parents on a child's success in school. Use specific reasons and examples to support your answer.

You should write at least 250 words.

I cannot completely agree with the statement that classmates are a more important influence than parents on a child's success in school. In this essay, I will first focus on the reasons why I agree with this statement and then list a few points, why from my opinion in some cases this is not true.

From the one side, classmates have a significant influence on a child's behaviour and his or her success in school. First of all, children spend much time at school. Classmates have many things in common, such as age, interests, homework and classes after all. So, they discuss their impressions about a new teacher, solve problems together, learn their homeworks, gain new knowledge and experience and even make their own discoveries. Sharing all these makes them closer. Some of them become friends and they spend after-school time together. In addition, friends tend to copy each other's habits and manners. For instance, my little sister became friends with the girl who did not have good grades at school at that time. It does not mean she could not have better grades; she just had many friends who did not care about their grades. So, when they began to spend their time together and share their interests, the girl's grades improved. They did their homework together, shared their dreams and exciting moments. From this point, I must agree that classmates can definitely change a child's attitude towards school.

On the other hand, parents too have a great influence on children' successes in school. For example, if parents show due interest in their child's progress and talk to him or her about the importance of learning, I think their child will listen to them and do his or her best.

Personally, I believe that relationships between parents and a child play an essential role in a child's success in school. If these relationships are close and wholehearted, I am sure that parents should not be afraid of bad influence from the outside.

TOPIC NO. 19

IMPROVE THE ISOLATED LIVES OF CITIES

You should spend about 40 minutes on this task.

With the increasing number of people in cities, most do not know their neighbours and the sense of community is lost. What is causing this? How can we turn it around?

You should write at least 250 words.

The life of people in the city, unlike in the countryside, is generally characterised by a lack of community feeling. A number of reasons can be attributed to this tendency among city dwellers. This situation can be addressed effectively if certain proactive steps are taken by the urban population. One of the major reasons for the isolated lifestyle in cities is the busy schedule of people due to extended working hours and long commuting time. To explain it further, many business firms in cities demand their employees to work beyond the usual hours owing to heavy traffic congestion getting to and fro from work is a time consuming affair. Even at home, people need to be engaged in their household chores, which leave them with hardly any time to interact even with their immediate neighbours.

Furthermore, the ethnic, cultural and linguistic diversity of people in cities, who come from different parts of a country or even other nations, does create serious hurdles for easy socialisation. For instance, in a city like Bangalore presently Bengalura, in India, people from all parts of the country who speak different languages live in the same apartment building. This makes it difficult for them to interact easily with each other.

An ideal way to deal with this problem is to encourage people to visit their neighbours on weekends and make friends with them. For example, occasionally, people who live next door can be invited for dinner or a special occasion, which can improve the interaction with them. Joining neighbourhood cultural forums and charity groups is another effective method to create a sense of community among the city dwellers. For example, families that live in apartments or housing colonies can form associations and meet occasionally to work for the welfare of the neighbourhood. Finally, using a common language like English for communication is also every useful. Such initiatives can definitely enhance a sense of unity and increase socialisation among people who live in cities.

TOPIC NO. 20

SHOULD EDUCATION BE FREE?

You should spend about 40 minutes on this task.

All education, primary, secondary and further education, should be free to all people and paid for by the government. Do you agree or disagree with this statement?

You should write at least 250 words.

The opinion that every citizen should have the right to study at school or university for free is a very controversial one. Those, who disagree, refer to the enormous expenditures of the government in case of establishing such laws. Although, I hold the viewpoint that not charging people for education could become very beneficial for the country and its economy.

Firstly, young people from poor families could be very smart. Looking back to history and biographics of distinguished people, raised in poverty can illustrate this best. Making schooling available only for fortunate is not fair. Moreover, the state well-being could also be affected, because there would be a lack of talented specialists, whose skills were not discovered and developed by proper training.

Another advantage of making education free of charge is happiness of the nation. Inability of individuals to collect the required amount of money needed to pay school or university fees causes stress and anxiety of the middle-class society, which can even keep them from having children. Nowadays, we can see that the lowest birthrate is in countries where prices of enrollment to higher education institutions are very high. This clearly indicates the fact that citizens of rich countries are generally not able to provide their future offsprings proper education.

Finally, nothing seems to be more beneficial to economy than an intelligent nation. Free courses and study programs can prepare excellent specialists, who would work to bring profit themselves and hence their respective countries. That would surely compensate most expenses of the state budget caused by education of no charge.

To sum up, even though making all schools free can be very expensive for the state economy, advantages are invaluable. After several years, such improvements would bring fruits of happiness, and an intelligent nation confident about its future.

TOPIC NO. 21

CAN TV TEACH PEOPLE?

You should spend about 40 minutes on this task.

Some people say that television is a very useful tool when it comes to education. Others argue that television is a much overused, ineffective teacher.

Discuss both of these views and give your opinion as to the usefulness of television as an educational tool.

Give reasons for your answer and include any relevant examples from your own knowledge or experience.

You should write at least 250 words.

There is a lot of controversy about whether TV can play a role as a teacher. Some people hold a viewpoint that it can never be educational at all. Others, although, disagree, referring to TV's high potentials of teaching through amusement.

As a matter of fact, television nowdays, can hardly be called educational. All those talk shows and soap operas, we can see every day are completely wastage of time and can even have negative effects by distracting young and disciplined people from their studies. Moreover, most of the so called educational programmes like the National Geographic Channel can not replace books and academic lectures because they tend to entertain people and not have an aim to give deep and concentrated knowledge.

Hovever, TV can be a powerful means of delivering information and an effective part of the learning process. Educational methodologists have proved that more senses are involved at the time of studying, the more effective results can be achieved. Television produces both picture and sound, so its usefulness is obvious. Many teachers already use this facility actively by showing students audio/video cassettes which go as supplementary material to many language courses. So why not broadcast such movies through television?

The problem of ineffectiveness of television as educational tool is in fact, not a problem of the television itself, but of people who decide the content of a particular channel. It is hardly unlikely that content directors would abandon their high profits and change the talk shows to lectures and video-lessons. Therefore, those, who insist on TV's uselessness maybe right, but let us not forget that as technology improves, new cheap ways of broadcasting, for instance, video podcasts have also come up. They can prove to be an exclusive power of learning tool, such as the television.

TOPIC NO. 22

WHO LEARNS LANGUAGES BETTER – CHILDREN OR ADULTS?

You should spend about 40 minutes on this task.

Some people think children are more successful in studying foreign languages than adults. Discuss.

You should write at least 250 words.

The viewpoint that children are better learners become almost a common sense, although it is not always true in terms of learning foreign languages.

When it comes to make an approach to, for example, Japanese or French, adults have proven themselves superior learners because of their experience of getting knowledge of their own language and their performance is generally better motivated.

Every adult has some amount of education it their past and it means he she has already received a general understanding of the structure of a native language. Thus, this more or less categorised base usually serves as a template for foreign grammar or vocabulary. A person only has to place new materials on certain shelves in his memory and operate them like their own language. Children, in contrast, are usually confused by any grammar, even of their own country. Bringing foreign language to curriculum adds embarrassment because they do not have sufficient understanding of grammatical or semantic categories and cannot bring to order such huge amounts of information.

Grown-ups also appear to be more enthusiastic about language studies. As a matter of fact, this skill for them is a tool that can be used to achieve career goals. Obviously, more motivated individuals do better, and even if his/her abilities are modest, through practice, success can come very fast and lot of success stories can prove it. Kids, though, usually consider second language lessons as fun or, otherwise, something boring and, even if they tend to absorb knowledge like sponges, without use, it rapidly disappears. With no proper encouragement, youngsters just do not know they have to practise new words and grammar in order not to forget them.

Thus, while, it would not be a mistake to suggest children are naturally better learners, let us not forget that adults are usually better suited to language studies.

TOPIC NO. 23

STUDYING & WORKING TOGETHER

You should spend about 40 minutes on this task.

Some people think high school graduates should travel or work for a period of time instead of going directly to study at the university.

Discuss the advantages and disadvantages of both the approaches.

Give reasons for your answer and include any relevant examples from your own knowledge or experience.

You should write at least 250 words.

There is a considerable controversy about what young people should do after receiving graduation certificate of the high school. The majority holds the viewpoint that obtaining an university degree immediately after school is the only option to become successful and an established person. Others, however, tend to disagree; in their opinion after finishing school, an individual should receive an opportunity to see the world or try his/her skills on job.

On one hand, the basic knowledge, that comes into possession of a pupil at school should be preserved and receive futher development at the university. Human brain forgets facts rapidly, especially those, which are not in use. In the case of making a long pause between graduation from school and enrolling to a university, the person may become unable to pass the admission exams.

On the other hand, on job training may provide an opportunity of receiving experience and choosing career before deciding the sphere, in which student wants to obtain higher education. For instance, a young person can try his skills of management, working as an assistant manager in a small shop. In addition, that could also help him to understand if this work is really what he desires and prevent from making an expensive mistake of choosing a wrong field.

Another option of understanding someone's needs is travelling. This is a perfect way to see the world and different professions in use. A person, who has never been in rural areas could be charmed, for example, by the romanticism of cheesemaking and come to a decision to make genuine milk products all his life.

To sum up, there are some ways different from the standard scheme of going to the university right after school and they should not be overlooked. Personally, I think that whichever option a person chooses, time before the university should not be wasted on entertainment or parties. It is essential to use it wisely, thinking about the future.

TOPIC NO. 24

THE PROBLEM OF WASTE

You should spend about 40 minutes on this task.

Nowadays, we are producing more and more rubbish.

Why do you think this is happening?

What can governments do to help reduce the amount of rubbish produced?

You should write at least 250 words.

In our highly industrialized era, there is a growing awareness about the excessive amounts of trash people are producing. We are about to be flooded by different types of garbage if certain measures are not taken.

To begin with, different food producers decided that their products will be selling better if they will pack them in small-sized boxes and packets. These colourful and attractive packs go straight to the trash can, and the number of packs are growing along with the consuming growth.

More consuming produces more waste. Government and businesses encourage more consumption because it leads to high profits and development of the state economy. They are not interested in the situation whether a person is going to use something for a long time. Society is being bombarded with commercials, pleading to buy, for instance, a new mobile phone. Buying new things cause throwing away the old, even good things.

The problem of garbage is very complicated. As we can see, the government is not interested in reducing consumption. Thus, the responsibility has to be taken by the individuals and the non-governmental organizations. Certain laws, regulating the percentage of packaging material per ton of product should be established. Moreover, interesting programs, involving people to participate can be developed. For example, bonuses for not asking for a plastic bag in supermarkets or for buying extra large packs of food.

In addition, everyone should become concerned about the future of human beings and our planet. If we do not wish to be buried in rubbish, we should think twice before buying things we do not need.

TOPIC NO. 25

DO INFORMATION TECHNOLOGIES LEAD TO SOCIAL PROBLEMS?

You should spend about 40 minutes on this task.

The age of Information Technology has taken a lot of people by surprise. While it has become a way of life for some, others know very little about it and may be unlikely to learn. Eventually, we will have a polarised society and this will lead to serious social problems.

To what extent do you agree with this statement?

You should write at least 250 words.

Our highly informatized era has become shock for many of us. At the time one part of society uses new means of information very actively, the other people stay in the dark without any chance to make an approach to understanding new technologies. There is a rising awareness of this problem which have a potential danger of slicing the society into two parts which would never understand each other.

It is a fact that many of our everyday activities became available for computer users only. For example, if you are a university student, you are supposed to submit your term paper as typed and printed document, they no longer accept hand written papers. Furthermore, some manufacturers do not distribute information leaflets, but give a website address of their products'on packs. Thus only the Internet users can have an access to the product details. The last but not the least, computer skills became a crucial requirement for employment in urban areas. The IT sector has completely convert the society into a polarised one. It makes the individual more isolated than into networking. Those who comprehend with the world of technology can be connected with each other, but for those whom everything is Greek lead an isolated life.

For example, the inhabitants of rural areas do not need new means of acquiring information. Their work and everyday activities do not demand using computers. For example, a farmer can use radio to hear news and ordinary mails to communicate.

Taking into account the fact that not every citizen can use new information technologies, governments would not change the traditional ways of interaction with their people. It is very much unlikely that people would no longer have a possibility to vote by filling papers by hand or do other activities, important for their citizenship.

Informatization of society affected those, who have a need of instant information exchange. People, whose lifestyle do not require any haste in communication have an opportunity to use traditional ways. I am assured that as long as situation does not make others to change their way of life against their will, there is no risk of facing serious social problems – Writing Essentials

TOPIC NO. 26

ANIMALS: TO USE OR NOT TO USE?

You should spend about 40 minutes on this task.

Animals should not be used for the benefit of human beings, unless there is evidence that animals do not suffer in any way.

To what extent do you agree or disagree with this statement?

You should write at least 250 words.

There is a lot of controversy about using animals for human needs. Animal rights activists are trying to stop all modern and traditional activities, which involve killing animals or cause their suffering. Traditionalists are trying to convince the community that using living creatures for men's needs is natural and cannot be avoided in everyday life.

Activists, who defend animal rights, are telling the world that people should not use animals in any way. Moreover, they say that animals should have exactly same rights as humans do. The reason is that people and animals are both living creatures and there shouldn't be any difference in treating them. There are some extreme vegetarians who refuse to eat any food of animal origin, even milk or honey. They try to convince people to do the same using as an argument that killing animals and keeping them in captivity cause their suffering and it's not a civilized action.

Traditionalists disagree with the statement that humans should stop killing animals or using them to fulfill their needs. From the very beginning of human civilization, there is a tradition and vital need to use animals as food and their parts in traditional crafts. Without proteins and vitamins of animal origin, human body wouldn't receive all the nutrients it needs. Moreover, testing some medicines on animals already helped to fight many diseases people suffered from.

I think, people have the moral right to use animals to their benefit, to some extent. I am sure, we should not cause them to suffer and die for our fun. Although, using animals for food is natural for humans as a predator, but as civilized predators, we should make sure to use only humane ways of killing.

TOPIC NO. 27

SPACE RESEARCH OR FIGHTING DISEASES?

You should spend about 40 minutes on this task.

Governments around the world are spending billions in support of space programs. This money would be better spent on research in the improvement of human health.

To what extent do you agree or disagree with this opinion?

You should write at least 250 words.

There is an opinion that countries are spending a lot of their cash assets on space projects, while they should rather finance medical science sufficiently. Spaceships are flying all over the Universe and at the same time people are dying from AIDS or even flu. Is there any point of throwing money into the outer space?

On one hand, humans really have not fought many dangerous and highly contagious diseases. Moreover, industrialization and economical progress brought new diseases as a result of receiving more comfortable lives. Some of these lifestyle diseases diabetes, cardio-vascular problems, etc. In addition, launching just one space shuttle into the sky requires so many natural resources and brings so much pollution, which affects ecology a lot. That brings us new health issues, that need additional funding, which could be withdrawn from excessive payments for space research.

Moreover, scientists already have fund raising from commercial pharmaceutical companies. A lot of diseases have been fought in just last 100 years and there is an increase in the life expectancy of human beings. However, improved health and long life of human population leads to a new problem – overpopulation. Space research can help to find a new home for Earth's inhabitants. The last, but not the least, could be that who knows, there is a chance we may find on other planets a panacea for all diseases.

As for me, I am not a very healthy person and nor are my parents. However, if there is a one, very small chance, that something exciting will happen and astronauts will meet alien civilization on other planets, I would be happy that the government a considerable amount of money on space research. We have overcrowded our planet and there is so much of air and sound pollution that we should search for ways of expanding our habitat.

TOPIC NO. 28

COMPUTER GAMES OR OUTDOOR SPORTS?

You should spend about 40 minutes on this task.

Children today are too much dependent on computers and electronic entertainment. It would be better for them to be outside playing sports and taking part in more traditional pastimes than spending all day indoors.

Do you agree or disagree with this statement?

You should write at least 250 words.

Together with computerization of our society, there is a rising public awareness about kids, who spend too much time in front of personal computer or playing video games. What is best for children is to devote their free time to outdoor activities and conventional games or to be at home and entertain themselves with computers?

Some types of PC games can be very innovative and may contain huge educational potential. They can encourage children to develop researching skills and inspire them to learn new things. However, most of the video games are dumb-type, which develop nothing but button-pushing skills. Unfortunately, these games are usually highly addictive. Thus, they can cause the lack of physical activity and even serious mental diseases.

Outdoor games are always more beneficial for kids' health. They not only train them in terms if agility and endurance, but teach children to socialize and make friends. Moreover, they make them stronger because of fresh air, physical activity and exposure to the sunlight. Therefore, physical activity in the form of games and sports is must for the overall development of children.

I was not very outgoing and physically active kid and preferred rather to read than to play with others. Getting a computer brought more diversity for my leisure and study. It helped me to experience new emotions, learn new things, study English and meet interesting people online. An aptitude for high information technologies helped me to get a good job when I grow up. Therefore, I think parents should look to their child's personality in order to decide what is more appropriate. Finding good balance between electronic entertainment and outdoor games depends on parents' ability to identify what benefits their child best.

TOPIC NO. 29

ASSETS OF MODERN WORLD – BOON OR BANE

You should spend about 40 minutes on this task.

Computers, televisions and internet, these are some of the necessary assets in our contemporary world. It seems that the world without media sources would come to a halt instantaneously. Analyse the constructive and the destructive side of modern technology.

You should write at least 250 words.

Computers, nowadays are the major attractions in any market, like offices homes or businesses or stocks. It has definitely changed the world we live in. With invent of this magnificent device, people have realized the benefits of technology, which is to make lives easier and comfortable, in this technological era. Even if you ask a 3 years old child how to operate a computer, answer will definitely be positive.

Generally speaking, computers are helping our communities in numerous ways. People have become more aware of technology, resulting in increased cognizance. Computers are assisting us in factories where operations are completely autonomous. In offices, computers help us to manage our data and information. Thus, computers have actually changed our world.

According to some researches done in America, there have been reports that using computers are harmful to our wellbeing. According to annuals published back in 2006, working on computers for long hours continuously, can lead to stress and depression. In addition to that, people tend to gain weight as they work on computers all day long. Further more, working on computers for more than four hours can lead to decrease in eyesight. But this is not all, by the invention of internet; minors have an easy access to explicit materials online. In addition to that, E-mail frauds are all time at a high rate.

In my opinion, every technology has some benefits and some drawbacks, just like the medical pills which have side effects. It is our discretion because the choice is ours. It depends upon us, which side to choose from, the constructive side of technology or the destructive side.

TOPIC NO. 30

VIRTUES OF HUMANITY

You should spend about 40 minutes on this task.

All people glorify and enthusiastically talk about human virtues and morality, yet few people actually live up to them. What is your opinion? Do you agree or disagree?

You should write at least 250 words.

An accordance to the above parable about conversation and following human virtues and ethics I would like to quote a proverbs "Early to bed , early to rise makes a man healthy, wealthy and wise" which people say but don't follow. Do they really represent what we called human nature? Undoubtedly, they are not.

The answer is disparaging, and depreciating in the true sense in a pragmatic way. These garrulous, so called high profiled people, lack principles themselves. They can be considered as the quintessence of incorrigible liars. The examples of these people can be found everywhere, take for instance, an esteemed politician, they know how to convince people at the time of voting, but after elections, where are those promises, moralities and merits. Their talk is really a pretence, but do they really apply all to themselves? Another example can we had of those people who talk about banning fashion shows as it is not up our intrinsic worth, but in reality, they are the one who watch these with full propagation. The question here arises that where is the morality then, only in words?

Exceptions are always there, no interrogations in it, but exceptions are rare. Statistics indicate the out of 100 people, approximately, 85 are not following what they are saying to others. So where is the morality, only in lectures? This tradition simply indicates that we are camouflaging our weaknesses over our sins.

In the nutshell, we can say that if forgiveness is divine, why people are giving capital punishment to others? People talk about human merits and principles but they themselves don't practise what they preach, isn't it disgusting? They live on the rules that rules are for others not for themselves. In my opinion, these people are a disgrace/stigma to the society.

TOPIC NO. 31

TEACHING OF FOREIGN LANGUAGE FROM CHILDHOOD

You should spend about 40 minutes on this task.

Should foreign languages be encouraged from kindergarten?

You should write at least 250 words.

Nothing concrete can be had without *aspiration, inspiration,* and *perspiration* Language is a mode of communication by which we can express our ideas, emotions, etc. on a piece of paper or otherwise. Apart from the native languages taught in schools and allied institutions I strongly feel that foreign languages should be encouraged from the kindergarten itself.

To illustrate my above mentioned viewpoint, I would like to quote some examples. As we often know that children are the backbone for any developing nation. So if they are strong the nation will progress. If they know foreign languages, they won't face any difficulty whenever they go abroad, and hence, will understand their culture and technology well. Secondly, we often talk about the world, which we consider as a global village bonded by one single theme, *love*. So encouraging foreign languages from the kindergarten itself will promote this theme, as the students/professionals won't have any misconception regarding other language.

To support my viewpoint further, I would like to add that promoting foreign languages from the beginning will help student learn new things, and they will develop themselves into well-defined professionals and citizens. Even society will acknowledge them as urban elites. This will bring an ingenious attitude in them. They won't be feeling guilty if they come to face such a situation called language barrier. Moreover, this boosting of foreign language at the kindergarten stage will generate a feeling of oneness and may simulate foreign currency growth.

In a nutshell, I can say that language (written, oral or symbolic) is the sole way to express yourself. So encouraging foreign language will not bring additional burden to children or kindergartens, but this will really help in proliferating their career and undoubtedly, strengthen a nation's stronghold, apart from generating the feeling of oneness.

TOPIC NO. 32
BAN ON SMOKING

You should spend about 40 minutes on this task.

Smoking in public places should be banned, what is your viewpoint, do you agree or disagree?

You should write at least 250 words.

Ban on smoking in public places is not only justified, but also imperative. Many countries are realizing the dangers of passive smoking and are coming up with measures to curb the problems popping up with *passive smoking*.

Medical science has fully supported the dangers of potential passive smoking. To illustrate my point I would like to cite the fact that most of the people die due to *cigarette smoking* which contains *nicotine*. Ingrained smokers pack up themselves with *lung and oral cancer* rather than from natural causes. The government is squandering astronomical sums for the treatment of pulmonary cancers and educating the populace of the dangers of smoking. The imposition of high taxes on nicotine based products has already been done to restrain this habit.

The debatable point is that to what extent these steps have been succeeded to dissuade the smokers. Cigarette smoking not only pollutes the air, but also makes the non-smokers inhale the stale smoke imperilling their health too. Ingrained smokers are not destroying their own health but also of others. The main critical issue in this respect is that is anyone (child or adult) safe from passive smoking? Even pregnant women can, if well imagined too.

Some smokers argue that banning smoking in public places is a direct impingement of their human rights but this line is futile because right to smoking is not absolute, but right to life is. Many persons unintentionally, take up smoking by watching others; thereby unleash the smoke in public places. This is what they call fashion.

Thus, it is imperative to impose appropriate laws as it will not only prevent the non-smokers from falling victim to the dangers of passive smoking, but also directly benefit the diehard smokers who would then have no choice but to curtail their smoking habit.

TOPIC NO. 33
DIGNITY OF WOMEN

You should spend about 40 minutes on this task.

Societies that don't respect and honour their women can never make progress. To what extent do you agree or disagree on this statement?

You should write at least 250 words.

Behind every successful man, there is a woman. In fact, this statement can be generalized for a state, country or a nation. Also that a country can never make progress if it doesn't respect their women counterparts.

The prologue of this statement can be attributed to simple questions: How will you distinguish between a civilized and uncivilized person or in fact, a developed or an underdeveloped nation? Can one answer this question by saying or referring to one's economic status or one's rank? Well, unfortunately, it is no. The answer declines in the reverence of their better halves. The society which commits atrocities on their weaker members is not only uncivilized, but also underdeveloped as referred to the developed and the civilized one's.

The brutalities done on women by men are not their sign of strength as they are construed as the sign of their weaknesses which they are camouflaging. Is the valour of men lies in committing crimes on the week and helpless women? The question is still debatable.

So why cant the societies who don't respect women progress, because the intelligence and wisdom of women is unique in every respect. By not acknowledging the efforts of women and depriving them of their rights means improper motherhood for future generations which hence weakens the society. *Margaret Thatcher*, *Mother Teresa*, *Florence Nightingale*, *Indira Gandhi*, etc. These names don't need any words to prove themselves, they were the torch bearers and had enlightened the lives of many. They represent the sublime face of self-service and sacrifice.

To conclude, I would like to say that women are the best gift ever gifted to man by God. Dishonouring and demoralising women folks will not only invite the wrath of God, but also disfigure him too. It is women who give birth to man, so how can he think of disrespecting the same and her progress simultaneously.

TOPIC NO. 34

PROBLEMS OF EVE TEASING AMONG JUVENILES

You should spend about 40 minutes on this task.

Today in this modern contemporary world, people are striving hard to earn their living and to have two square meals a day. In this so called high profiled technological growth, people are suffering from many problems and diseases. As the growth is proliferating so is the problem of maligning image. Today the juveniles are suffering from what is called eve-teasing.

You should write at least 250 words.

Eve teasing is scaling rapidly nowadays. As per the dictionary meaning of eve teasing it means commenting on a girl or a lady in order to make fun, or abashing her. This problem has elevated now as compared to the past. Question arises what is the main cause of eve-teasing? Is it that we want to show that we are superior to others? Or, we just want to make fun of others. Well whatever may be the reasons; this is really a bad aspect of human life that we are treating others as inhumane.

The problem of eve teasing may be attributed to the bad education scenario, because it is what the education makes the human as humane. Today's education scenario is such like we have some hesitation in talking to people of the other gender. We are not taught how to behave with the members of other gender. Another main factor which is contributing towards growing this menace is the fashion of today. Today fashion is such that we are automatically compelled towards eve teasing. As far as I am concerned, I think the cinema also is responsible for some part of eve teasing. Movies are not what they used to be earlier. They are disturbing the minds of people, affecting their mentality and growth. People are becoming stoical, not conventional. They are not of placating nature now. Last but not least social networking sites like *facebook, twitter, etc.,* provide licence to throw mud on any member of the society with their maligning comments on photos and status of any profile.

In a nutshell, we can say that eve teasing is a becoming a serious problem. People who undergo eve teasing may end up their life due to abashment. Therefore, government should behave like a martinet and should imprison or impose monetary implications on those who are responsible because everyone in this world has the right to live without trepidations and tensions.

TOPIC NO. 35
COMPLEXITIES OF HUMAN MIND

You should spend about 40 minutes on this task.

The human mind tries to find complex solutions to the simple problems. To what extent do you agree or disagree?

You should write at least 250 words.

Apropos to the above statement, I consider this as human nature. We are connoting westernization to such extent that we feel shameful if we look 'simple'. Remaining simple this may also be attributed to what is called out of fashion.

Why we have tied ourselves into so many kinds? Have we increased the complexities ourselves? In the retrospect, it was not so. People were simple and their lifestyle matching to them; so the problems were also simple. The mind, 'thoughts' accordingly.

The insight of this statement reveals the fact that we are 'addicted' to make mountain out of mole hill. The human nature is so complex that it makes complex solutions even to fairly easy problems. Even if there are no problems, the mind tries to generate one and then visualizes it making it complex. An old saying that "empty vessels make much noise" is quite apt in this situation.

To exemplify, I would like to give some examples. Suppose your food is not tasty, then mind starts thinking why it is not tasty and then it starts pondering over it making it a complex problem. Another instance can be had of overweight. Overweight, no doubt is a problem, but still the mind makes it more complex and you switch to weight loss, dieting techniques and taking pills instead of 'simply' exercising.

Furthermore, going on the same track, I would like to add the example of 'looks' which are 'euphermal' but for looks people are going to cosmetic or plastic surgeons for getting their face lifted and for removing wrinkles. Question arises why they or (human mind, in particular) doesn't understand the simple problem of ageing which is universal. Isn't it the complex solution to a fairly simple problem? Other examples may include weathering, insomnia, etc which are a natural phenomenon, but our mind tries to find complex solutions to even these natural and simple 'phenomena' and 'problems'.

TOPIC No. 36

PRIVATE *vs* GOVERNMENT INSTITUTIONS

You should spend about 40 minutes on this task.

> *Do you think that Private Institutions Should be Banned?* You should write at least 250 words.

Private institutions should not be banned. As by banning them, it will mean, abating the choices made by parents for the future of their children. They may not get best education and quality of studies in Government institutions. Hence, life for the bright students may be downsized. Furthermore, consequences could be devastating for the future of an individual and perhaps for the whole nation.

On the other hand, there will be a huge positive impact on the way our Government Schools work if the Private Institutions are banned. Once government institutions realize their problems and shortcomings, the quality of teaching and thc code of practice will improve. As the code of conduct improves in the Government Institutions, their way of teaching will be more pragmatic. Also there will definitely be profits from schools which will go in Government Treasury, once the private institutes are banned. Hence, the school conditions will improve. These schools will then retrospect the multi-religious culture and will teach students to be respectful towards other religions. Parents will definitely benefit from this decision by paying less tuition fees in Government institutions as compared to the Private Institutions. Furthermore, there will be a sense of equality between students and there will no rich or poor in schools.

Absence of private schools may become a source of anguish for the middle and high income people. It may be misunderstood as a loss in freedom of choice the Government has taken the right of choice from away parents for their children's or it may be considered that education.

Some of the children who need special education or attention need private education. For instance, people with disabilities will be cared more in private institutions for their needs as compared to the Government Institutions. Similarly, the blind the or deaf also need special attention and care which, in my opinion, is impossible to be provided in Government Institutions.

In nutshell, I would like to assert the importance of *Private Institutes* in our community. Private Institutions cater to the needs for all types of students. They always change their teaching styles and skills in accord to the demand of students, providing them with high standard of education. *So I strongly feel that private education should not be banned.*

TOPIC NO.37

MEDICAL PROFESSIONALS *vs* FILM ACTORS

You should spend about 40 minutes on this task.

Do you think that medical professionals and engineers must be paid more as compared to film actors?

You should write at least 250 words.

Apropos of the statement, I strongly believe that medical professionals and engineers must be paid more as compared to film actors. By pragmatic cognizance, one can understand that doctors and engineers are the buttress of our society and economy.

Doctors and nurses are individuals who not only work for a living, but also contribute to our society. They are the people who can be regarded as the "Hands of God". Reason being they save our lives, hence, make this planet a better place to live in. If one really wants to understand what it means to be a doctor, ask them, they will tell that you must have a "heart of a lion and hands of a weaver" in order to be a doctor. It is so true. Doctors and nurses improve our quality of lives. They contribute to the community in ways different to any other professions.

Similarly, teachers are also the building blocks of our society. They educate us in order to make us successful in our professional and personal lives. Mentors make us realize our true potential and our responsibilities as an individual. Personally speaking, they are the messengers of angels who teach us how our life should be. They give us a sense of direction in our lives. They show us the way to success.

Doctors, teachers and nurses are undoubtedly, the pillars of any nation. Therefore, it becomes imperative to understand that they must be paid well in order to help build our community not just for themselves, but for the whole society. Doctors and nurses should be paid according to their ranks and their departments. Higher the precision required, higher should be the pay. Similarly, teachers should be paid according to their rank and qualifications. And one most important thing is to increment their salaries every year to keep them motivated.

On the contrary to these professions, actors should not be paid huge amounts for their acting. Main reason being apart of showing their sexuality, emotions and their violent nature, they sometimes exhibit wrong ideas in our society. I feel they have a limited contribution to our community as compared to any other profession.

In a nutshell, I would like to assert that doctors, teachers and nurses should be paid well as compared to actors. The main reason is because doctors, teachers and nurses contribute to our society constructively. On the other hand, film industry at times, actually contribute destructively towards exhibiting necessary vulgarity and to our community.

TOPIC NO. 38

KEEPING PETS AT HOME

You should spend about 40 minutes on this task.

Do you agree with keeping pets at home? Give reasons in support of your answer.

You should write at least 250 words.

I am in consummate accord with this statement. There is too much attention on keeping a pet, even though people throughout the world are starving. However, one cannot avoid the benefits of keeping pets. Pets are known to bring harmony in the families and lives of people.

Pets are a source of happiness and recreation for people of all ages. Pets, especially dogs may keep a person fit, as it is important to take dogs for a walk. So, pets could be one of the reasons to stay fit. Guide dogs are helpful to our community. Everyone knows the significance of these specially trained dogs in the lives of blind pcople. Guide dogs act as eyes through which they see. Dogs are also known to save lives, in some cases. At night, dogs act like guards on patrol, saving our houses from burglars.

Although there are benefits to keep pets, but they could also be a source of various diseases. Viruses are known to be prescnt in animals and birds. By their droppings, these viruses can travel places, infecting people which could lead to deaths in the worst case scenario. Some pets, like cats and parrots can be aggressive and impulsive and it can result in instant attacks to people, which can be fatal too!

Loss of a pet can be devastating to family members, especially children. Pets have, tendency to blend as a family member, so their loss can create the same effect as a loss of a family member. As a consequence, it can lead to depression among young children in the family.

Having a pet could also mean a lots of additional expenditure too, or a burden to the family. It is up to a person, whether to keep a pet or negate the idea of having one. Once it is decided to get a pet, the foremost things to do is to manage the finances well in advance.

In the end, I would like to say that it actually depends upon a person, either to adopt a pet or give up the idea of having one. Personally speaking, I would like to have a dog in future, as I like to keep myself fit and I think it will enhance my lifestyle, in addition to the security reasons as dogs are known to guard our houses/assets very faithfully.

TOPIC NO. 39

SOURCES OF ENTERTAINMENT

You should spend about 40 minutes on this task.

Listening to radio is more enjoyable and practical than watching television. Do you agree or disagree with this statement?

You should write at least 250 words.

Listening to radio and watching television are both entertaining, but some people believe that watching television is not much fun and does not impart much information as listening to radio. I disagree with them because listening to radio cannot counter with watching television in many ways.

In the first place, television carries more information than radio. For example, people can watch programs, interviews and news with pictures and motions on television, whereas via radio, it is hard to tell what is happening by only using words. Those images and scenes on television not only can tell the story but they can also bring the audience closer to the story by showing them the real situation. As a rule, people can see the faces of the speakers on television, so that they know where those words come from. These kinds of information, in effect, make the activity of watching television more enjoyable and practical.

Another reason that I think listening to radio is not as good as watching television is that the programs on the television are usually more up-to-date than radio. For example, the broadcasting companies usually commit more resources to the latest news, while radio stations often lack the resources to find the information. In addition, radio stations also cannot afford to produce big shows to entertain people.

Despite of the advantages of watching television, there are some benefits in listening to radio which we cannot overlook. For example, a television is usually very large and is difficult to carry whereas, a radio is very convenient to carry while travelling. Under these circumstances, a radio is more practical and gives us more fun on our trips. In addition, the portability of a radio makes it a perfect choice to be with us, while we are doing other activities such as sports or studying.

In conclusion, although listening to radio may be enjoyable and practical in some situations, watching television is a better choice because of its rich information and its up-to-date feature. I believe that in the future, television might become smaller and replace radios.

TOPIC NO. 40

INTERNATIONAL ENTERTAINERS *vs* POVERTY

You should spend about 40 minutes on this task.

International entertainers, including sports personalities are often paid millions of dollars in one year. In your view, with widespread poverty in the world, are these huge earnings justified?

You should give reasons for your answer using your own ideas and experience.

You should write at least 250 words.

The salaries of many singers, dancers and sports people have increased out of all proportion in the recent years, while in places like Sudan, people are starving to death. I do not believe that anyone should be able to earn such enormous salaries when so many people in the world are living in poverty. One of the factors which should affect what a person can earn ought to be the benefit of person's work to the society. It is unreasonable for a famous singer to be able to earn far more from an evening's entertainment than, for instance, a medical scientist who develops a new drug which produces a treatment for a common disease. The pop star certainly has a value in society, but the value in no way exceeds, or even matches, the value gained from a successful medication.

Secondly, work done should be paid according to the amount of efforts and skills that go into it. Nobody would deny that a famous person works hard and is skilful, yet such people do not work any harder than thousands of other workers who have no claim to fame. Yet market force are such that these superstars can obtain millions of dollars, while other unknown people sometimes earn less than they need to survive. Finally, it should be the responsibility of the government to work together with private firms to ensure that the amount of money in circulation should be more equally and fairly distributed. This seems only fair given that there are so many sufferers. To conclude, it is clear that the world poverty is a serious problem and yet the problem can be erased if governments give more to the starving and less to the fully bellied people.

TOPIC NO. 41
EARNING OF WRITERS

You should spend about 40 minutes on this task.

Most writers of fiction do not earn enough money to live from their writing. Do you think the government should give them financial assistance to help encourage good literature?

You should give reasons for your answer using your own ideas and experience.

You should write at least 250 words.

There are some conditions under which a novelist could reasonably expect some government support. In general terms, if the writer has already proved that he or she can write well, and if the stories produced are stimulating and interesting, then I consider that some financial help might be given. Language quality is difficult to define, but if the writing shows, for example, good grammar, a wide vocabulary, and elegance and imagination, then I can see a valid reason for assisting an author to spend some time free from money problems. Such a writing needs to be encouraged. The entertainment value of a book should also be a factor in deciding whether to provide assistance to an author.

Further consideration should include social and educational values expressed in the author's work. However, if the ideas are socially irresponsible, or if the stories contain unnecessary violence or pornography for its own sake, then I would not want to see the author sponsored to write stories which do not benefit the society. Other exceptions are the many writers of good books who do not require financial help. Books which proved to be extremely popular, such as the *Harry Potter stories*, clearly need no subsidy at all because the authors have become rich through their writing.Views on what good quality writing means will vary widely and so if any author is to be given money for writing, then the decision would have to be made by a committee or panel of judges. An individual opinion would certainly cause disagreement among the reading public.

TOPIC NO. 42
PROBLEM OF SOCIALISATION

You should spend about 40 minutes on this task.

With the increasing number of people in cities, most do not know their neighbours and the sense of community is lost. What is causing this? How can we turn it around?

You should write at least 250 words.

The life of people in the city, unlike in the countryside, is generally characterised by a lack of community feeling. A number of reasons can be attributed to this tendency among the city dwellers. This situation can be addressed effectively if certain proactive steps are taken by the urban population. One of the major reasons for the isolated lifestyle in cities is the busy schedule of people due to extended working hours and long commuting time. To explain it further, many business firms in cities demand their employees to work beyond the usual hours and owing to heavy traffic congestion getting to and fro from work is a time consuming affair. Even at home, people need to be engaged in their household chores, which leave them with hardly any time to interact even with their immediate neighbours.

Furthermore, the ethnic, cultural and linguistic diversity of people in cities, who come from different parts of a country or even other nations, do create serious hurdles for easy socialisation. For instance, in a city like bengaluru in India, people from all parts of the country who speak different languages live in the same apartment or building. This makes it difficult for them to interact easily with each other.

An ideal way to deal with this problem is to encourage people to visit their neighbours on weekends and make friends with them. For example, occasionally people who live next door can be invited for dinner or a special occasion, which can improve interaction with them. Joining neighbourhood cultural forums and charity groups is another effective method to create a sense of community among the city dwellers. For example, families that live in apartments or housing colonies can form associations and meet occasionally to work for the welfare of the neighbourhood. Finally, using a common language like English for communication is also very useful. Such initiatives can definitely enhance a sense of unity and increase socialisation among people who live in cities.

PRACTICE ESSAY
WRITING TASK –2
(UNSOLVED)

1. Without capital punishment (the death penalty), our lives are less secure and crimes of violence increase. Capital punishment is essential to control violence in the society. To what extent do you agree or disagree with this opinion?

   Write at least 250 words.

2. "Fatherhood ought to be emphasised as much as motherhood. The idea that women are solely responsible for deciding whether or not to have babies leads to the idea that they are also responsible for bringing up their children."

3. Millions of people every year move to English-speaking countries, such as Australia, Britain or America, in order to study at school, college or university. Why do so many people want to study in English? Why is English such an important international language?

4. The mass media, including television, radio and newspapers, have a great influence in shaping people's ideas.To what extent do you agree or disagree with this statement? Give reasons for your answer.

5. 'Telecommuting' refers to workers doing their jobs from home for part of each week and communicating with their office using computer technology.Telecommuting is growing in many countries and is expected to be common for most office workers in the coming decades.

6. In some countries, the average worker is obliged to retire at the age of 50, while in others, people can work until they are 65 or 70. Meanwhile, we see some politicians enjoying power well into their eighties. Clearly, there is little agreement on an appropriate retirement age.

   Until what age do you think people should be encouraged to remain in paid employment? Give reasons for your answer.

7. Going overseas for university study is an exciting prospect for many people. But while it may offer some advantages, it is probably better to stay home because of the difficulties a student inevitably encounters living and studying in a different culture. To what extent do you agree or disagree with this statement? Give reasons for your answer.

8. In the past, buildings often reflected the culture of a society, but today all modern buildings look alike and cities throughout the world are becoming more and more similar. What do you think is the reason for this, and is it a good thing or a bad thing?

9. Popular events like the Football World Cup (FIFA) or Cricket Matches and other international sporting occasions are essential in easing international tensions and releasing patriotic emotions in a safe way.

10. People attend college or university for many different reasons (for example, new experiences, career preparations, increase knowledge, etc.) Why do you think people attend college or university?

SELF-IMPROVEMENT/PERSONALITY DEVELOPMENT

Also Available in Hindi

Also Available in Hindi

Also Available in Kannada, Tamil

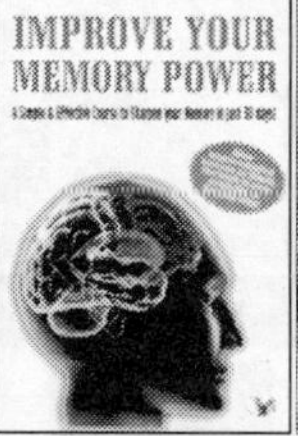

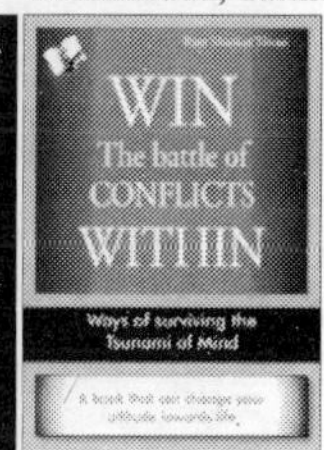

Also Available in Kannada

Also Available in Kannada

STRESS MANAGEMEN

All books available at www.vspublishers.com

HINDI LITERATURE

MUSIC/MYSTERIES/MAGIC & FACT

Also Available in Hindi

TALES & STORIES

NEW All Books Fully Coloured

OTHER BOOKS

Also available in Hindi

CHILDREN TALES (बच्चों की कहानियाँ)

BANGLA LANGUAGE (बांगला भाषा)

V&S OLYMPIAD GUIDE BOOK AND WORKBOOK SERIES (CLASSES 1-10)

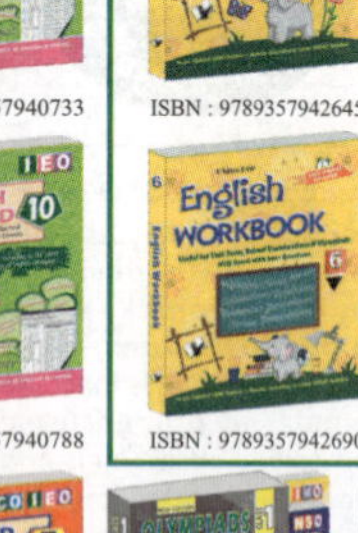

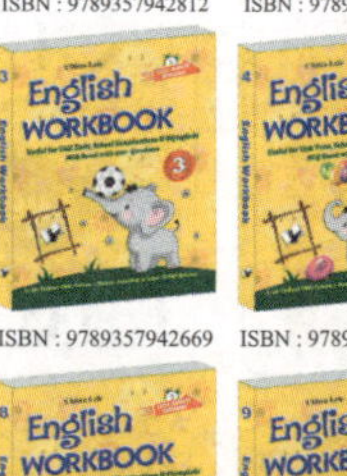

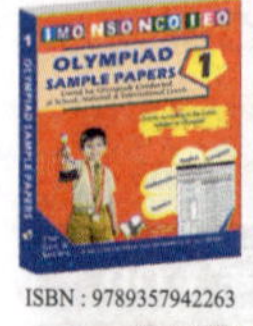

ISBN : 9789357940504 ISBN : 9789357940511 ISBN : 9789357940528 ISBN : 9789357940535 ISBN : 9789357940542 ISBN : 9789357942447 ISBN : 9789357942454 ISBN : 9789357942461 ISBN : 9789357942478 ISBN : 978935794

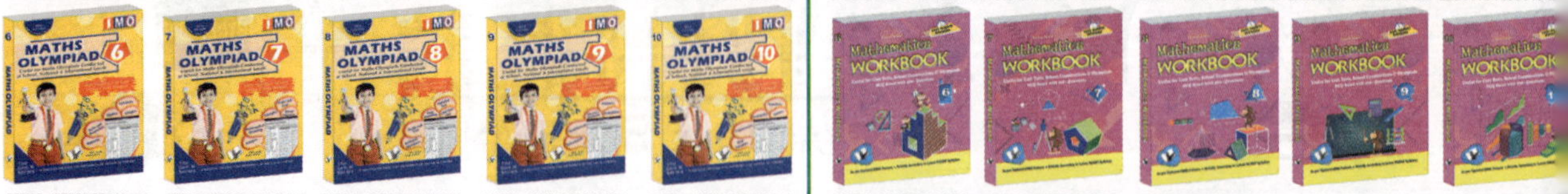

ISBN : 9789357940559 ISBN : 9789357940566 ISBN : 9789357940573 ISBN : 9789357940580 ISBN : 9789357940597 ISBN : 9789357942492 ISBN : 9789357942508 ISBN : 9789357942515 ISBN : 9789357942522 ISBN : 9789357942

ISBN : 9789357940405 ISBN : 9789357940412 ISBN : 9789357940429 ISBN : 9789357940436 ISBN : 9789357940443 ISBN : 9789357942546 ISBN : 9789357942553 ISBN : 9789357942560 ISBN : 9789357942577 ISBN : 9789357942

ISBN : 9789357940450 ISBN : 9789357940467 ISBN : 9789357940474 ISBN : 9789357940481 ISBN : 9789357940498 ISBN : 9789357942591 ISBN : 9789357942607 ISBN : 9789357942614 ISBN : 9789357942621 ISBN : 978935794

ISBN : 9789357942102 ISBN : 9789357940603 ISBN : 9789357940610 ISBN : 9789357940627 ISBN : 9789357940634 ISBN : 9789357942744 ISBN : 9789357942751 ISBN : 9789357942768 ISBN : 9789357942775 ISBN : 978935794

ISBN : 9789357940641 ISBN : 9789357940658 ISBN : 9789357940665 ISBN : 9789357940672 ISBN : 9789357940689 ISBN : 9789357942799 ISBN : 9789357942805 ISBN : 9789357942812 ISBN : 9789357942829 ISBN : 978935794

ISBN : 9789357940696 ISBN : 9789357940702 ISBN : 9789357940719 ISBN : 9789357940726 ISBN : 9789357940733 ISBN : 9789357942645 ISBN : 9789357942652 ISBN : 9789357942669 ISBN : 9789357942676 ISBN : 978935794

ISBN : 9789357940740 ISBN : 9789357940757 ISBN : 9789357940764 ISBN : 9789357940771 ISBN : 9789357940788 ISBN : 9789357942690 ISBN : 9789357942706 ISBN : 9789357942713 ISBN : 9789357942720 ISBN : 978935794

ISBN : 9789357942263 ISBN : 9789357942270 ISBN : 9789357942287 ISBN : 9789357942294 ISBN : 9789357942300 ISBN : 9789357942003 ISBN : 9789357942010 ISBN : 9789357942027 ISBN : 9789357942034 ISBN : 978935794

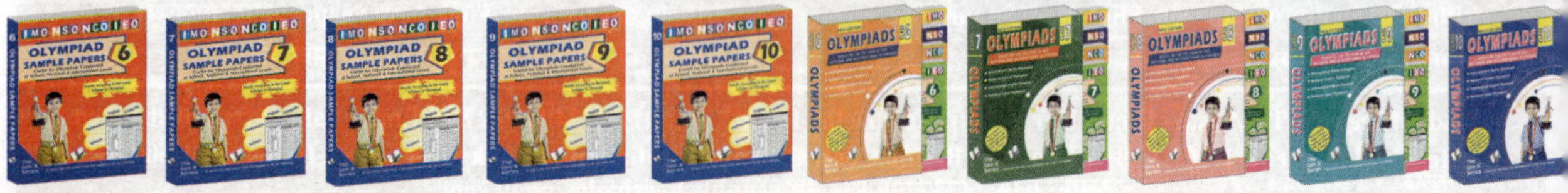

ISBN : 9789357942317 ISBN : 9789357942324 ISBN : 9789357942331 ISBN : 9789357942348 ISBN : 9789357942355 ISBN : 9789357942058 ISBN : 9789357942065 ISBN : 9789357942072 ISBN : 9789357942089 ISBN : 978935794

CAREER & BUSINESS/SELF-HELP/PERSONALITY DEVELOPMENT/STRESS MANAGEMENT

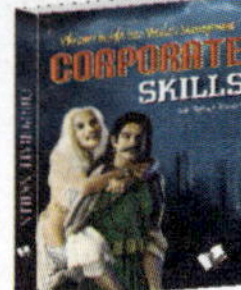

ISBN : 9789381588789 | ISBN : 9789350571637 | ISBN : 9789381588512 | ISBN : 9789381588963 | ISBN : 9789381588598 | ISBN : 9789381384039 | ISBN : 9788192079622 | ISBN : 9789350570753 | ISBN : 9789381384396

SBN : 9789381384541 | ISBN : 9789350570968 | ISBN : 9789381384527 | ISBN : 9789381588666 | ISBN : 9789381384541 | ISBN : 9789381384107 | ISBN : 9789350571187 | ISBN : 9789381588574 | ISBN : 9789381588277

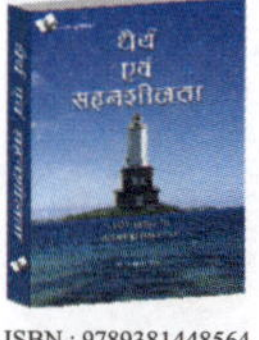
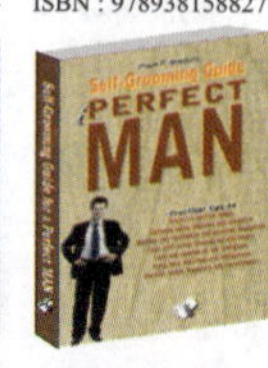

ISBN : 9789381588222 | ISBN : 9789381384213 | ISBN : 9789381588772 | ISBN : 9789381588949 | ISBN : 9789357940108 | ISBN : 9789381384152 | ISBN : 9789381384145 | ISBN : 9789381448564 | ISBN : 9789381384473

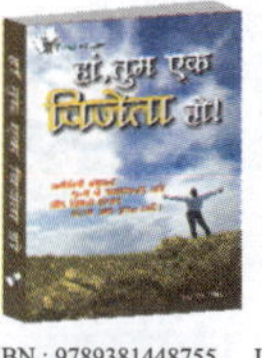

ISBN : 9789381448595 | ISBN : 9789381448670 | ISBN : 9789381588253 | ISBN : 9789381448755 | ISBN : 9789381448649 | ISBN : 9789381384480 | ISBN : 9789350571309 | ISBN : 9789381448632 | ISBN : 9789381384893

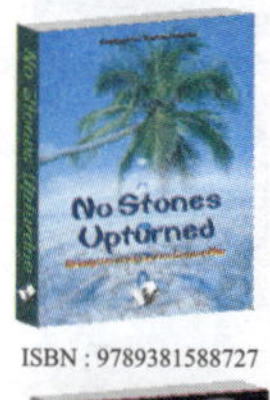

ISBN : 9789381384091 | ISBN : 9789381384176 | ISBN : 9789350570265 | ISBN : 9789381588727 | ISBN : 9789350570128 | ISBN : 9789381588246 | ISBN : 9789381448687 | ISBN : 9789381448786 | ISBN : 9789381448533

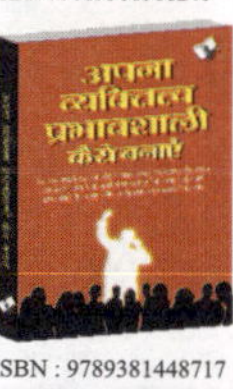

ISBN : 9789381448526 | ISBN : 9789381384206 | ISBN : 9788122310689 | ISBN : 9789381384503 | ISBN : 9789381588505 | ISBN : 9789381448717 | ISBN : 9788192079646 | ISBN : 9789350570203 | ISBN : 9789350570272

ISBN : 9789381588741 | ISBN : 9789350571170 | ISBN : 9789381588215 | ISBN : 9789381384763 | ISBN : 9789350570296 | ISBN : 9789381588284 | ISBN : 9789381588543 | ISBN : 9789350571880 | ISBN : 9789381588765

ISBN : 9789350570579 | ISBN : 9789350571927 | ISBN : 9789350571545 | ISBN : 9789381384114 | ISBN : 9789381384435 | ISBN : 9789381448779 | ISBN : 9789381448991 | ISBN : 9789381384510 | ISBN : 9789381384169 | ISBN : 9789350570623

ISBN : 9789381448908 | ISBN : 9789381448915 | ISBN : 9789381448922 | ISBN : 9789381448939 | ISBN : 9789381448946 | ISBN : 9789357940795 | ISBN : 9789357940801 | ISBN : 9789357940818 | ISBN : 9789357941303 | ISBN : 9789357941853

STUDENT LEARNING/QUIZ/POPULAR SCIENCE/BIOGRAPHIES

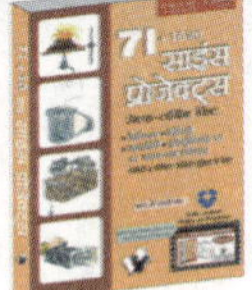

ISBN : 9789357941310 ISBN : 9789357941495 ISBN : 9789381384053 ISBN : 9789381384060 ISBN : 9789381384121 ISBN : 9788122310924 ISBN : 9789381588468 ISBN : 9789381588604 ISBN : 9789350570494

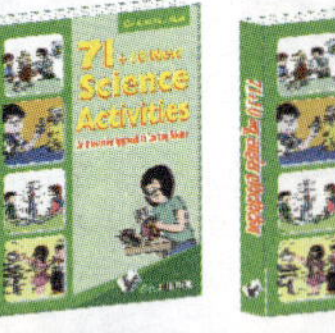
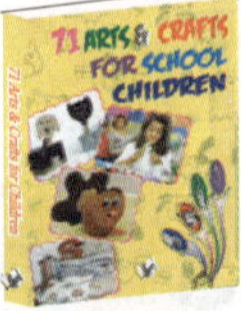

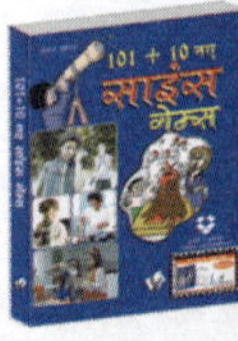

ISBN : 9789350570470 ISBN : 9789350570487 ISBN : 9789350570500 ISBN : 9789350570586 ISBN : 9789350571248 ISBN : 9789350571248 ISBN : 9789350571743 ISBN : 9789381384299 ISBN : 9789381448052

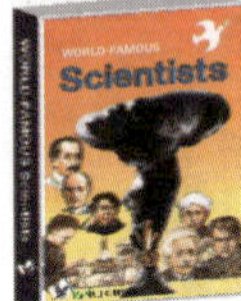

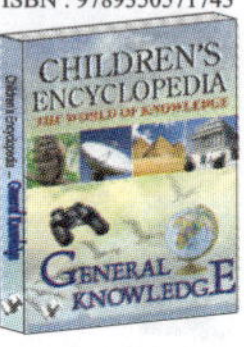

ISBN : 9789381384305 ISBN : 9789381384954 ISBN : 9789381588819 ISBN : 9789350570371 ISBN : 9789350570388 ISBN : 9789350570395 ISBN : 9789350570401 ISBN : 9789350570364 ISBN : 9789381588444

ISBN : 9789381448977 ISBN : 9789381384459 ISBN : 9789381384930 ISBN : 9789350571682 ISBN : 9789381588864 ISBN : 9789381588673 ISBN : 9789350570111 ISBN : 9789381384312 ISBN : 9789381588680

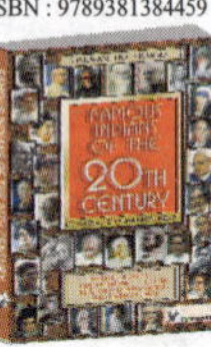

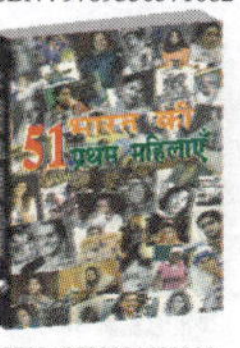

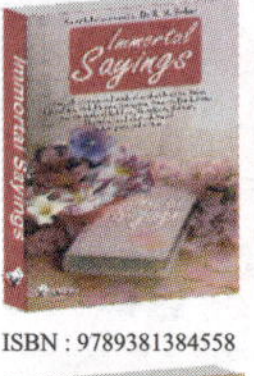
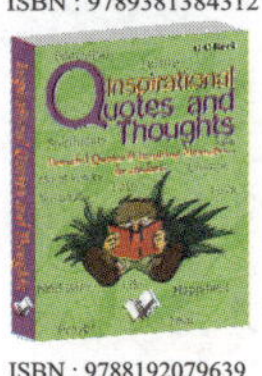

ISBN : 9789350570258 ISBN : 9789350570227 ISBN : 9789381588499 ISBN : 9789381588338 ISBN : 9789381588345 ISBN : 9789381448656 ISBN : 9789381384558 ISBN : 9788192079639 ISBN : 9789350571019

ISBN : 9789350571026 ISBN : 9789350571033 ISBN : 9789350571040 ISBN : 9789350571057 ISBN : 9789350570999 ISBN : 9789350571002 ISBN : 9789350571064 ISBN : 9789350571071 ISBN : 9789350571088

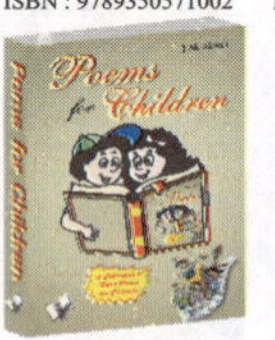

ISBN : 9789350571101 ISBN : 9789381588321 ISBN : 9789381588307 ISBN : 9789381588567 ISBN : 9789350571163 ISBN : 9789350570517 ISBN : 9789381384183 ISBN : 9789381448625 ISBN : 9789381384794

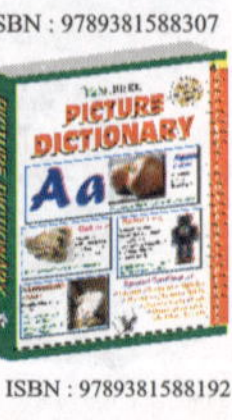

ISBN : 9789381384190 ISBN : 9789381448793 ISBN : 9789381588192 ISBN : 9789381588802 ISBN : 9789381588970 ISBN : 9789350570777 ISBN : 9789381448427 ISBN : 9789350570555 ISBN : 9789350570548

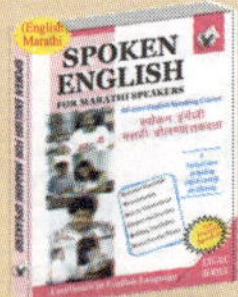
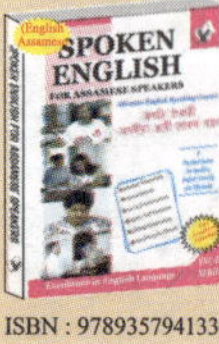
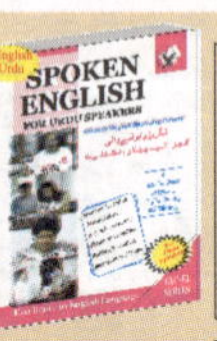
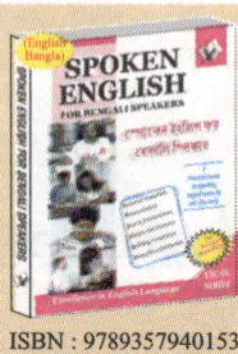
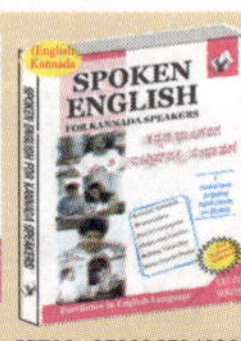
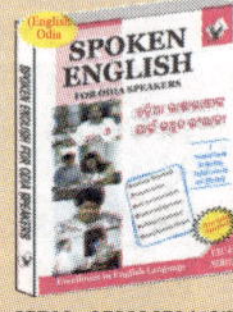
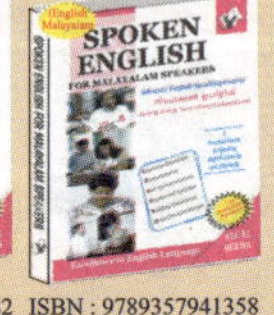

ISBN : 9789357940856 ISBN : 9789357940849 ISBN : 9789357941334 ISBN : 9789357941341 ISBN : 9789357940153 ISBN : 9789357940399 ISBN : 9789357940375 ISBN : 9789357940382 ISBN : 9789357941358 ISBN : 978935794132

FICTION/FUN & FACT, TALES & STORIES/LEISURE READING

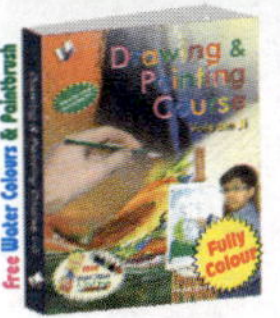

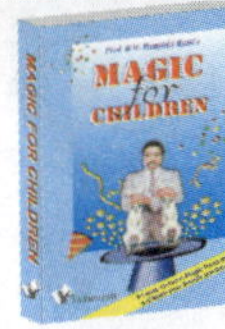

ISBN : 9788192079660 ISBN : 9788192079677 ISBN : 9789381588659 ISBN : 9789381588840 ISBN : 9789381588857 ISBN : 9789381588871 ISBN : 9789381588888 ISBN : 9789381384336 ISBN : 9789381448069

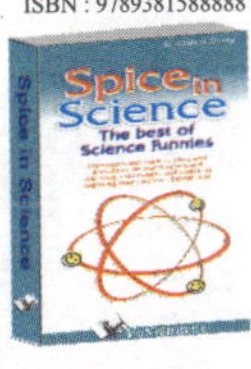

ISBN : 9789381448090 ISBN : 9789381448083 ISBN : 9789381384343 ISBN : 9789381448076 ISBN : 9789381448809 ISBN : 9789381448885 ISBN : 9789350571248 ISBN : 9789350570210 ISBN : 9789381384329

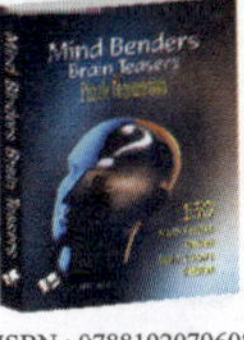

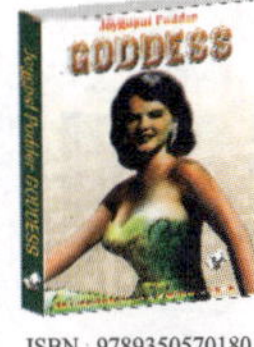
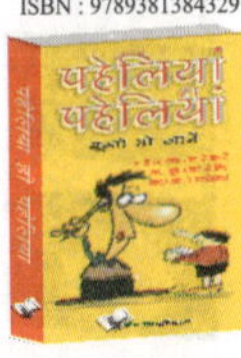

ISBN : 9789381448229 ISBN : 9789381448236 ISBN : 9789350570227 ISBN : 9789381588697 ISBN : 9788192079608 ISBN : 9789350571644 ISBN : 9789381588734 ISBN : 9789350570180 ISBN : 9789381448168

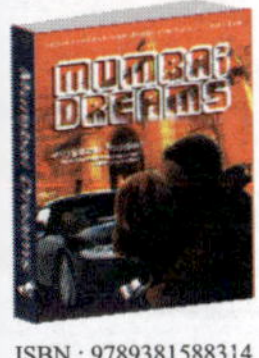

ISBN : 9789381588314 ISBN : 9789381588260 ISBN : 9788192079691 ISBN : 9789381588291 ISBN : 9789381588956 ISBN : 9789350570852 ISBN : 9789350570906 ISBN : 9789350570838 ISBN : 9789350570883

ISBN : 9789350570845 ISBN : 9789350570890 ISBN : 9789350570869 ISBN : 9789350570913 ISBN : 9789350570821 ISBN : 9783950570876 ISBN : 9789350570920 ISBN : 9789350570937

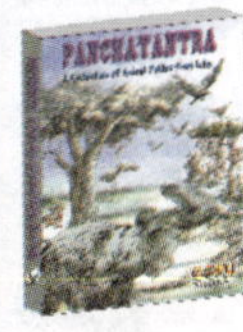

ISBN : 9789381588987 ISBN : 9789350570005 ISBN : 9789350570012 ISBN : 9789350570029 ISBN : 9789381588994 ISBN : 9789350570036 ISBN : 9789350570043 ISBN : 9789350570050 ISBN : 9789381588406 ISBN : 9789350571552

ISBN : 9789381448182 ISBN : 9789381448199 ISBN : 9789381448144 ISBN : 9789381384404 ISBN : 9789381588451 ISBN : 9789381588581 ISBN : 9789381588529 ISBN : 9789381448137 ISBN : 9789381448106 ISBN : 9789381588178

ISBN : 9789381448175 ISBN : 9789381448113 ISBN : 9789381448120 ISBN : 9789381448151 ISBN : 9789381384701 ISBN : 9789381384718 ISBN : 9789381384862 ISBN : 9788192079615 ISBN : 9789381384015 ISBN : 9789381588185

ISBN : 9789350570760 ISBN : 9789350570098 ISBN : 9789350571699 ISBN : 9789350571125 ISBN : 9789357940146 ISBN : 9789357940139 ISBN : 9789350571620 ISBN : 9789350571118 ISBN : 9789350570982 ISBN : 9789350571835

HEALTH & BEAUTY CARE/FAMILY & RELATIONS/LIFESTYLE

ISBN : 9789350570463 ISBN : 9789381588482 ISBN : 9789381448724 ISBN : 9789381448762 ISBN : 9789381448823 ISBN : 9789381384961 ISBN : 9789381384442 ISBN : 9789381448496 ISBN : 9789381588918

ISBN : 9788122307511 ISBN : 9789381448502 ISBN : 9789381384633 ISBN : 9789381448489 ISBN : 9789381384251 ISBN : 9789350570593 ISBN : 9789381384831 ISBN : 9789381384800 ISBN : 9789350570616

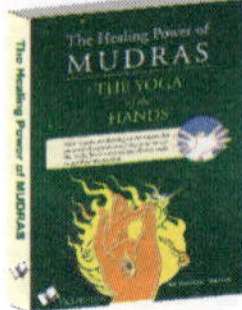

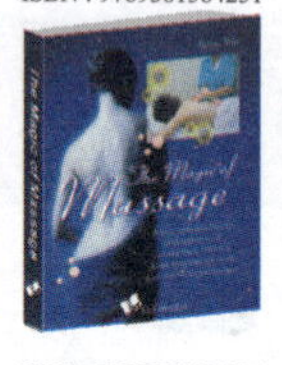

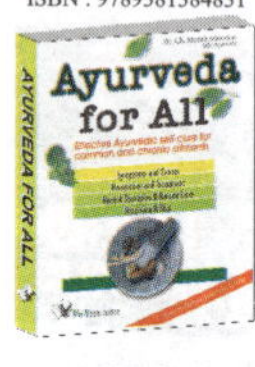

ISBN : 9789381384220 ISBN : 9789381384817 ISBN : 9789381384572 ISBN : 9789381448694 ISBN : 9789381384824 ISBN : 9789381384565 ISBN : 9789381384909 ISBN : 9789350570609 ISBN : 9789381448663

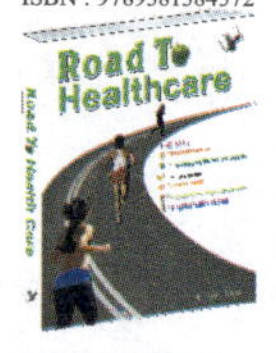

ISBN : 9789381448458 ISBN : 9789381384589 ISBN : 9788192079653 ISBN : 9789381384978 ISBN : 9789381448472 ISBN : 9789381448731 ISBN : 9789350571897 ISBN : 9789381448434 ISBN : 9789381448465

(also available in Hindi)

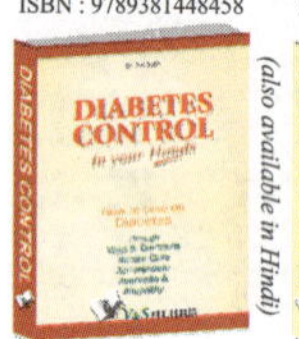

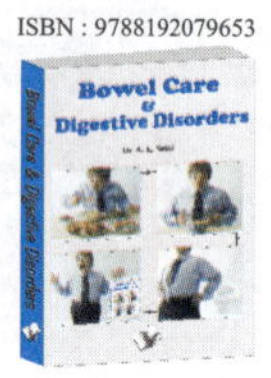

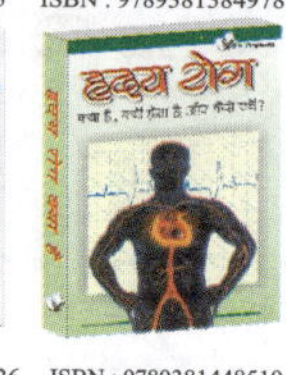

ISBN : 9789381384244 ISBN : 9789381384237 ISBN : 9789381384626 ISBN : 9789381448519 ISBN : 9789381384619 ISBN : 9789381448892 ISBN : 9789381384602 ISBN : 9789381588369 ISBN : 9789381588376

ISBN : 9789381588383 ISBN : 9789381588390 ISBN : 9789381448557 ISBN : 9789381588826 ISBN : 9789381384268 ISBN : 9788122305159 ISBN : 9789381448748 ISBN : 9789381384992 ISBN : 9789381384664

ISBN : 9789381448700 ISBN : 9789381588758 ISBN : 9789381384923 ISBN : 9789350570104 ISBN : 9789381448618 ISBN : 9789381448441 ISBN : 9789381384688 ISBN : 9789381384282 ISBN : 9788122308808

ISBN : 9789381448854 ISBN : 9789381384046 ISBN : 9789381384275 ISBN : 9789381384985 ISBN : 9789381448601 ISBN : 9789381448861 ISBN : 9789381384640 ISBN : 9789381384848 ISBN : 9789381384657

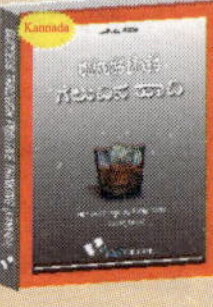

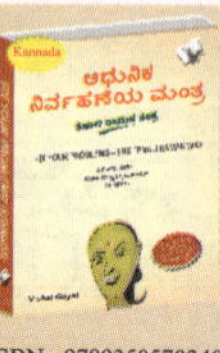
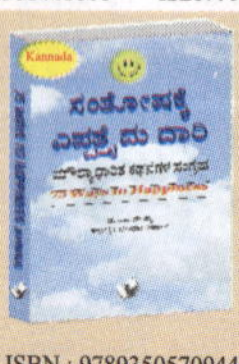
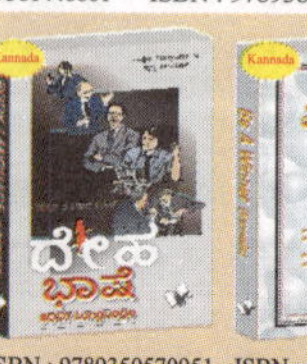

ISBN : 9788122310924 ISBN : 9789357940078 ISBN 9789350570357 ISBN : 9789350571200 ISBN : 9789350570340 ISBN : 9789350570944 ISBN : 9789350570951 ISBN : 9789350571309 ISBN : 9789350571828 ISBN : 9789350571781

SUBJECT DICTIONARIES/IELTS/ACADEMIC/COMPUTER LEARNING

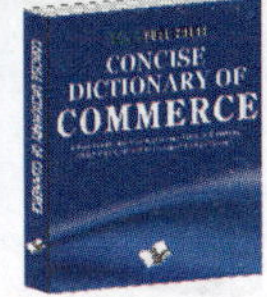
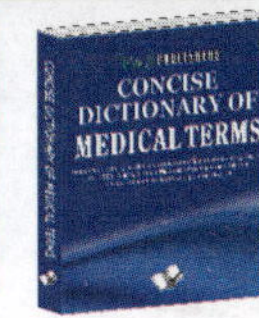

ISBN : 9789350571576 ISBN : 9789350571583 ISBN : 9789350571606 ISBN : 9789350571590 ISBN : 9789350571613

ISBN : 9789381588611 ISBN : 9789381588628 ISBN : 9789381588642 ISBN : 9789381588635 ISBN : 9789381588833 ISBN : 9789350570326 ISBN : 9789350570319 ISBN : 9789350570333

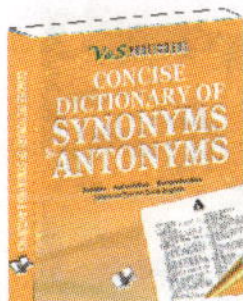
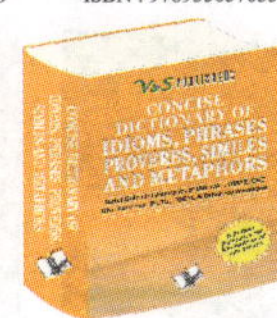

ISBN : 9789350571507 ISBN : 9789350571491 ISBN : 9789350571521 ISBN : 9789350571453

ISBN : 9789350571224 ISBN : 9789350571231 ISBN : 9789350571460 ISBN : 9789350571453 ISBN : 9789350571484 ISBN : 9789350571477 ISBN : 9789350571668 ISBN : 9789350571538

ISBN : 9789350571392 ISBN : 9789350571385 ISBN : 9789350571408 ISBN : 9789350571330 ISBN : 9789350571347

ISBN : 9789350571415 ISBN : 9789350571439 ISBN : 9789350571422 ISBN : 9789350571361 ISBN : 9789350571354 ISBN : 9789350571378 ISBN : 9789350571149 ISBN : 9789350571330

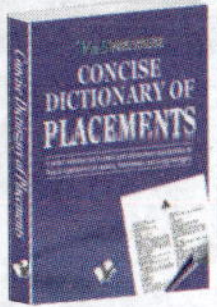

ISBN : 9789357942232

ISBN : 9789350571651 ISBN : 9789350571286 ISBN : 9789350571255 ISBN : 9789350571262 ISBN : 9789350571293 ISBN : 9789350571279 ISBN : 9789350571569 ISBN : 9789357940368 ISBN : 9789350571934

ISBN : 9789357942379 ISBN : 9789357942256

ISBN : 9789350571705 ISBN : 9789350570241 ISBN : 9789350570234 ISBN : 9789350571965 ISBN : 9789357941365 ISBN : 9789357941549 ISBN : 9789357941556 ISBN : 9789357941563 ISBN : 9789357941570

ISBN : 9789357942386 ISBN : 9789357942249

ISBN : 9789357941501 ISBN : 9789357941518 ISBN : 9789357941525 ISBN : 9789357941532 ISBN : 9789357941747 ISBN : 9789357941716 ISBN : 9789357941709 ISBN : 9789357941723

ISBN : 9789357942393 ISBN : 9789357942225

ISBN : 9789357941730 ISBN : 9789350571693 ISBN : 9789357941655 ISBN : 9789357941662 ISBN : 9789357941679 ISBN : 9789357941686 ISBN : 9789350570173 ISBN : 9789381588895

ISBN : 9789357942362

ISBN : 9789350570142 ISBN : 9789381588536 ISBN : 9789350570159 ISBN : 9789350570128 ISBN : 9789350571316 ISBN : 9789350571989 ISBN : 9789350570135 ISBN : 9789350570166

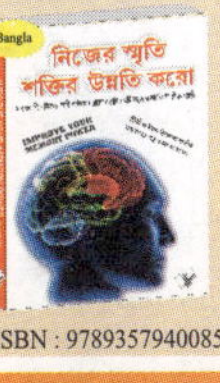

ISBN : 9789357940054 ISBN : 9789357940016 ISBN : 9789357940023 ISBN : 9789357940085 ISBN : 9789357940825 ISBN : 9789357940092 ISBN : 9789357940009 ISBN : 9789357940030 ISBN : 9789357940061

ASTROLOGY/PALMISTRY/VAASTU/HYPNOTISM/RELIGION & SPIRITUALITY

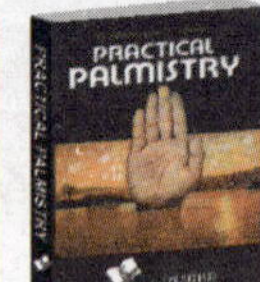

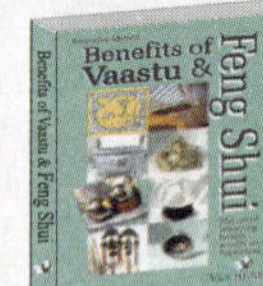

ISBN : 9789381588925 ISBN : 9789381588710 ISBN : 9789381448540 ISBN : 9789381448045 ISBN : 9789381384350 ISBN : 9789381384367 ISBN : 9789381384077 ISBN : 9789357940832 ISBN : 9789381384534

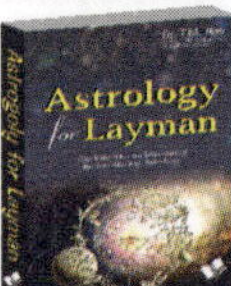

(also available in Hindi)

ISBN : 9789381384374 ISBN : 9789350571194 ISBN : 9789381384466 ISBN : 9789381448021 ISBN : 9789381448014 ISBN : 9789381588796 ISBN : 9789381588796 ISBN : 9789381384084 ISBN : 9789381448212

ISBN : 9789381384756 ISBN : 9789381384879 ISBN : 9788122309973 ISBN : 9788122310849 ISBN : 9789381384497 ISBN : 9789381384886 ISBN : 9789381384497 ISBN : 9789381448878 ISBN : 9789381384725

NEW ARRIVALS

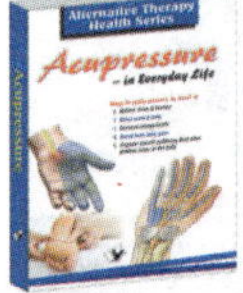

ISBN : 9789357941471 ISBN : 9789357941457 ISBN : 9789357941419 ISBN : 9789357941433 ISBN : 9789357941464 ISBN : 9789357941402 ISBN : 9789357941396 ISBN : 9789357941389 ISBN : 9789357941372 ISBN : 9789357941488

ISBN : 9789357941440 ISBN : 9789350571842 ISBN : 9789350571859 ISBN : 9789357942843 ISBN : 9789357941938 ISBN : 9789350571958 ISBN : 9789350571941 ISBN : 9789350571132 ISBN : 9789350571767 ISBN : 9789350571774

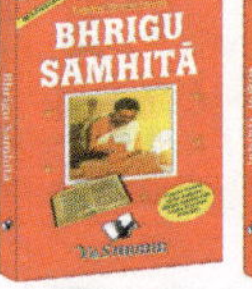

ISBN : 9789350571750 ISBN : 9789357941426 ISBN : 9789357941860 ISBN : 9789350571903 ISBN : 9789350571910 ISBN : 9789357940207 ISBN : 9789357940214 ISBN : 9789357940221 ISBN : 9789350571972 ISBN : 9789357940177

ISBN : 9789357940184 ISBN : 9789357940191 ISBN : 9789381384770 ISBN : 9789357942850 ISBN : 9789357941983 ISBN : 9789357941990 ISBN : 9789357940313 ISBN : 9789357940320 ISBN : 9789357941976 ISBN : 9789357941969

ISBN : 9789357940306

ISBN : 9789357940276

ISBN : 9789357940283

ISBN : 9789357940290

ISBN : 9789357951873

ISBN : 9789357941866

ISBN : 9789357940269 ISBN : 9789357940238 ISBN : 9789357940245 ISBN : 9789357940252 ISBN : 9789357941952 ISBN : 9789357941945

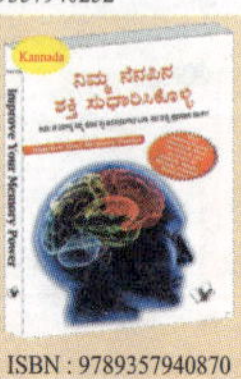
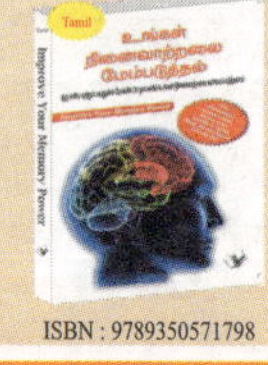

ISBN : 9789357940047 ISBN : 9789350571811 ISBN : 9789350571804 ISBN : 9789381384138 ISBN : 9789381384121 ISBN : 9789357940870 ISBN : 9789350571798 ISBN : 9789357940863 ISBN : 9789357942409